Confessions of a

CHELSEA BOY

Spencer Matthews was born in Grantham, but largely brought up on St Barths, where his parents own the glamorous Eden Rock hotel. He went to school at Eton, where he spent a lot of time in the headmaster's office.

After studying film at the University of Southern California in LA for a year, he went to work as a City broker and a club promoter for famous London venues like Boujis, Movida and Amika.

A member of the hit show *Made in Chelsea* since it began in 2010, Spencer was also the star of Channel 5's *The Bachelor* in 2012. He blogs for the Mail Online.

Confessions of a
CHELSEA BOY

SPENCER MATTHEWS

PAN BOOKS

First published 2013 by Sidgwick & Jackson

First published in paperback 2014 by Pan Books
an imprint of Pan Macmillan, a division of Macmillan Publishers Limited
Pan Macmillan, 20 New Wharf Road, London N1 9RR
Basingstoke and Oxford
Associated companies throughout the world
www.panmacmillan.com

ISBN 978-1-4472-4270-3

1 3 5 7 9 8 6 4 2

A CIP catalogue record for this book is available from the British Library.

Typeset by Ellipsis Digital Limited, Glasgow
Printed by CPI Group (UK) Ltd, Croydon, CR0 4YY

Visit **www.panmacmillan.com** to read more about all our books
and to buy them. You will also find features, author interviews and
news of any author events, and you can sign up for e-newsletters
so that you're always first to hear about our new releases.

For our brother Michael

Some of the author's proceeds from this book
have gone to the Michael Matthews Foundation.

Contents

Prologue

'And the BAFTA for best Reality and Constructed Factual TV Show goes to . . .'

There was complete silence in the Royal Opera House as the audience waited for Holly Willoughby to reveal the winner. I had been waiting for this moment ever since being told that *Made in Chelsea* was nominated for the second year running. Although we faced stiff competition from *The Young Apprentice*, *I'm A Celebrity* and *The Audience*, deep down I felt that we could beat them. After five series, the show was still going from strength to strength.

When we arrived at the red carpet the amount of press and paparazzi coverage was overwhelming. There were hundreds of flashing lights going off at once and all the faces around me were familiar. Everyone had made a real effort. The dresses and heels were splendid, the suits were Bond-like. I'd grown up watching many of these people on television and in movies, and now I was walking among them; competing even.

Now, sitting with my friends from the show, our eyes glued to Holly as she opened the envelope, I lost all confidence. The BAFTA would surely elude us once again. It was too good to be true.

Then, as fate would have it, and to what appeared to be Holly's delight, she announced, '. . . *Made in Chelsea*!'

The feeling was one of overpowering emotion. One of my dearest friends, Jamie Laing, shared a moment with me that would last a lifetime – we fell in love all over again – it was like we'd achieved everything that we had set out to.

Once on stage, Francis Boulle and I managed to ad-lib a speech. People were thanked and we drew particular attention to the fact that *Made in Chelsea* is a time-consuming production that employs many people and that it is an honour to be recognized by such a distinguished panel. Winning this statue is like receiving a British Oscar, and is the most critically acclaimed award we could receive.

'Who knew you could get a BAFTA for being posh!' Francis amusingly ended on.

Some people were happy for us, some felt robbed, some were indifferent, which I suppose is normal of any awards ceremony. However, what really gave us a sense of overwhelming achievement on this night was that history had been made. *Made in Chelsea* had become the first show of its kind to win a BAFTA judged by the panel.

The press interviews passed rather seamlessly, and then it was off to the afterparty where we certainly didn't hold back. The BAFTA statues ended up in an ice bucket when not being used as cricket bats. Jamie was bowling ice – few people were hurt. The evening as a whole was such a special occasion, and even those whom I'd had my differences with on the show became close friends, if only for a night.

Having always wanted to work in film or television, it was certainly the most rewarding moment of my career to date. But at times it does concern me that people believe the bubble that is *Made in Chelsea* is the entirety of my life rather than just a part of it. It is true that I am from what many call a privileged background but, more importantly, I had an incredible upbringing in a loving family imbued with a strong work ethic and an equally strong sense of fun. It is true that doors were opened for me offering opportunities that I am aware many others would not have had, but that doesn't mean my life has always gone smoothly. I've experienced heartbreaking loss and made mistakes I regret. Of course, I have also had some amazing adventures, including the time when the US Embassy was believed to be under attack by me and sent an armed rapid response unit to apprehend me, and a couple of near-death experiences, first in a rally race, later in a powerboat race. Then there's the memorable occasion when I managed to insult Colonel Gaddafi's son and was hunted round St Barths by a couple of his more dangerous-looking men – there was a beautiful girl involved. There's usually a girl involved . . .

I hope this book will show you that there is more to me than meets the eye and that the lovable rogue you may love or loathe means well.

CHAPTER 1

Meet the Matthews Family

As a boy, being naughty was a fun pastime for me and I was very good at it. Luckily, Caunton Manor, where I spent my early years, offered plenty of scope to a boy with a lot of imagination and a penchant for mischief.

Caunton Manor is a gorgeous eighteenth-century country house located just outside the market town of Grantham in Lincolnshire. To a small child the house looked magical, with its stone columns and rows of big windows. In one of the outbuildings there was a large dance floor which, at the flick of a switch, would rise to reveal a pool. Thirty acres of land included gardens, woodland and a go-karting track. Having acquired the house in 1986, Mum and Dad restored the glasshouses, which were filled with figs, vines and salad greens, and added barns, pony paddocks and a trout pond. We kept dogs, chickens, sheep and pigs and would release a few pheasants too. It was the perfect place in which to grow up.

But before I tell you any childhood stories, let me first

introduce the most important people in my life: my mum Jane, dad David – not as it turns out the lead singer from The Dave Matthews Band but hereafter in the book (as in life) called The Band by me – my brothers James and Michael, and my sister Nina. My parents are open and honest, and believe that work is paramount. To this day I can tell them anything. They encouraged us as children, punished us if really necessary, but rarely preached. They often disapprove of the way I behave as an adult, but they support me and do what they can to urge me back in the right direction. They know that even when I've taken a wrong turn, I do usually mean well.

The Band has a great work ethic as well as entrepreneurial flair. He was born in 1943 to parents Wallace and Eunice, and – along with his brother Bob, who was one year older – grew up in the village of Thurcroft near Rotherham. It was a typically happy Yorkshire childhood and The Band becomes ever so slightly animated when he talks about playing cricket against a dustbin and the way people would safely leave their doors unlocked. Of course, as a Yorkshireman he also approves of the local habit of straight talking . . .

Grandpa Wallace had a harder time growing up. He and his older brother Richard were thrown out of the house together, in wintertime, by their new stepmother when Grandpa was fifteen. He survived by travelling round the coalfields of England and Wales doing jobbing work. During his thirties, Grandpa Wallace set up in business in Yorkshire contracting for underground jobs in the coal industry. Later he branched out a bit and became involved in other small businesses in the Thurcroft area. One of these interests was Kingsforth Garage, which sold four different types of petrol from four different old pumps and did car repairs. On leaving school, this was where The Band would start work as an apprentice car mechanic, attending Sheffield Technical College one day a week – which he didn't much enjoy, he says. This distaste for academic work was a trait he passed down to at least one of his three sons.

Grandpa Wallace died before I was born, but Grandma Eunice is fit and well, and at the time of writing is ninety-four and still independent. With strong help from family and friends, she is battling on towards receiving a telegram from the Queen when she scores her first century.

At nineteen, The Band started to sell cars door to door in the backstreets of Rotherham and Sheffield, and became interested in motor racing. He bought an insurance write-off 1959 Mini for £35, then rebuilt it and club raced successfully on the northern circuits in 1965/6. Then Dad met Kevin MacDonald, a successful local industrialist and fellow motor-racing enthusiast, and they became close friends. Kevin and his wife Donna are my godparents. Dad began driving Kevin's two very good racing cars in 1971/2, and their Melton Racing Team won British national events, with Dad becoming division champion in the British Touring Car Championship in both years.

The Ford Motor Company began to support the Melton Team and, when their contracted professional driver was killed in France in a Formula Two race in early 1973, The Band was offered a full-time professional job driving for Ford UK to test and race their cars. In August that year he was caught up himself in a violent high-speed accident when competing in a support race at the British Grand Prix at Silverstone. One driver lost his life and another one, Dave Brodie, was badly injured when his car was launched high into the air and landed back down on fire. Dad's car was destroyed as it end-over-ended at 130 mph. The doors flew off and the seat came out but the fire extinguisher system kicked into action and the six-point seat belts held, so he was flying around half in and half out of the car. His heart stopped due to the centrifugal shock but was restarted easily enough, he says. Apart from that he suffered few serious injuries other than damage to his left eye, which continues to this day and ended his motor racing career.

He reapplied himself to business and, helped by a small team of cheerful, robust and very hard-working Yorkshire folk – some of whom remain friends after all these years – assembled Kirkby Central Group, which in 1987 became a public company after reversing itself into Plaxton PLC, the celebrated Scarborough-based luxury motor coach maker. A reverse takeover is when a smaller business persuades a larger one to acquire it, then, by agreement, the management from the smaller company moves straight through to lead the enlarged business. A similar acquisition was made into Henly's PLC, the national motor dealer and finance business, and the whole group briefly entered the UK stock exchange top 500 companies. Throughout all this activity The Band was chairman and chief executive of the whole business. In 1991 he left the group and began specializing in property development, often working alone or with a small group of people and always operating as a private company.

I love my father and I do see a lot of similarities between the two of us. He's not so sure! We both like people, and we both enjoy change and action and moving forward, but I would definitely say he's more hard-working than I am.

Before he met Mum, Dad was briefly married to someone else who, if pressed very hard, he will describe simply as 'charming on her day'. The one wonderful thing that came out of this first marriage is my half-sister Nina, who is, and always has been, absolutely lovely. She's twenty years older than me, although you wouldn't know it because she looks like Sharon Stone at her best – say in *Basic Instinct*.

Nina lived with us at Caunton Manor for a while and she pampered me a great deal. She loved to chat and play and there was never any problem about us having different mothers. Nina is just as important to me as my brothers are.

Meanwhile, Mum grew up in Rhodesia (now Zimbabwe) and at eighteen was voted Carnival Queen by her fellow undergrads at Rhodes University in South Africa. She rode through the town on a motorized float, on her throne, with her two nifty handmaidens hanging on for dear life as the clutch of the float truck was a bit sharp. I'm not surprised she was voted into the job, as she is as gorgeous now as she was then, with her sun-kissed hair, a petite and beautifully structured face and a slender frame. Now in her sixties, she's often mistaken for someone in her forties and I'm proud to have her on my arm when we toddle off shopping together.

But there is far more to Mum than her stunning looks. She was good at most sports, including tennis, and she finished runner-up in the Zimbabwe under-fifteen Mashonaland Championships. Her love of sport possibly came from her father, Robert Spencer Parker, who played rugby for Central Rand and occasionally for the national team. 'Spenny' Parker also founded the Stragglers Cricket Club in Rhodesia, whose teams were open to all races, i.e. anyone who loved the game. As is often said, there's nothing much wrong with people who love cricket. Grandpa Spenny was a talented architect who designed the high court in Salisbury (now Harare) and the library, as well as a number of schools and many interestingly styled domestic houses. Mum tells me that he was a wild character who enjoyed a drink and had, er, memorable social skills.

Spenny would devote many happy hours to drinking in the Salisbury Club and pubs, without needing to put his hand in his pocket – not that he was tight, he just had a useful talent. He'd sketch clever cartoons and caricatures of the other drinkers present, handing them round freely to roars of laughter. The drinks would flow, the party would come alive and race away – and no doubt very often mischief would ensue at the end of the evening.

I never got to meet Spenny unfortunately – he died suddenly in 1980, having barely suffered a day of illness in his life beforehand – but my parents, who were moved to name me after him, say that I am Robert Spencer Parker reincarnated. Drinking, mischief, out every night, social skills, ladies, and a love of art . . . what on earth do they mean? I'm sorry not to have met Spenny Parker. From what I can tell from the family, we'd have been great friends.

Mum has always found family genes fascinating – and Spenny passed a few of his artistic ones her way. Mum's love of painting and sculpture – but not cartoons – gained her a place at Rhodes University, where she studied Fine Art and achieved a diploma with distinction in painting. In 1968 she won the Purvis Prize for best painter of the year, which carried with it a scholarship to the Rijks Academy in Amsterdam. Waved off from the docks in Cape Town by her loving mother Doras, her stepfather Cy, her beloved sister Pamela and brother Paul, she set sail for Europe aboard the *Union Castle* ocean liner, her destination London. She planned to have a quick look-see at the city before making her way to Amsterdam, but as it turned out, she wasn't to leave the UK for many years.

At twenty-one, she moved to London and into a flat on Redcliffe Road in Chelsea, and had various jobs before landing the post of receptionist at Christian Dior. Not long after that, she met The Band, who had first seen a photograph of her on the carnival float when his sister-in-law Lu (an ex-Rhodes graduate too) was flicking through an old university yearbook. Dad, who was living alone at the time with his Labrador Groucho, tracked down Mum's number and called her. For some reason he decided it would be a good idea to tell her that he had red hair and wore heavy glasses – unsurprisingly, the joke backfired and Mum refused to see him. He called her one last time and finally got her to agree, in a lukewarm kind of way, to meet with him. They met at Redcliffe Road and when she saw Dad, it was love at first sight. And it wasn't just because he had turned up in his Ferrari Daytona. In fact, she says she was so struck by him that she didn't even notice the car, even though they walked past it on their way to the famous Old Finch's pub with its sawdust floors round the corner on Fulham Road. But then Mum's never been much fussed about material things.

From that moment on, the two of them were inseparable and their families were convinced that they'd be married swiftly. Mum popped back to Rhodesia briefly, and on her return to the UK they moved into their first home together – Dad's bungalow 'Lakeside', in Lindrick Dale in Yorkshire. As for marriage, Dad is not the kind of chap to make a fuss and perhaps also felt some unease about tying the knot again, so there was no going down on one knee. Turns out when they were to be married, Mum didn't even know . . .

The story is that they were both a little bit hungover from a party the night before, and Mum remembers being dressed in an old brown sweater and skirt, expecting a quiet day at home. Dad claimed to be busy as usual and asked her to come with him to Rotherham town centre so she could park the car while he nipped in and out of his meetings more easily. The next thing Mum knew she was parked outside a building and Dad was asking her to jump out quickly and come with him for a couple of minutes. They were at the register office and twenty minutes later out they walked, married! Despite the fact that The Band's confidence has rubbed off on me in many ways, I'd probably do this differently.

After the ceremony they went back to Bob and Lu's house. They were in on the game and had laid on some celebratory champagne. Mum called her mother in Rhodesia, who was surprised but delighted. However, she did say, 'Do be careful. Those racing drivers do rip it up a bit!'

After just one glass of champagne, The Band went back to work. Not the most romantic of stories, I'll grant you, but Mum says she was happy with the way Dad had surprised her. And don't worry, Cinderella did go to the ball when she and The Band enjoyed a spectacular wedding party in Rhodesia with all of the energetic and good-humoured Parker family and their entertaining friends, drinking and dancing into the night. Apparently Grandpa Spencer turned up two hours late, on a donkey.

Mum became pregnant quite soon afterwards and my brother James was born on 21 August 1975. Eighteen months later our brother Mike joined the family. I followed some twelve years after when Mum was forty-two, and despite always suspecting that I was a mistake, Mum swears that wasn't the case. The family had recently moved from Lindrick Dale to Caunton Manor, about twenty miles away, and Mum and Dad felt the bigger house would benefit from being home to a larger family – and along I came.

I was born on 6 August 1988 and was so overdue, punctuality never being never my strong point, that when I finally presented myself, I weighed a pretty colossal 9 lb. Mum recalls that I refused to cry but a firm spank from the doctor did the trick. Turned out to be the first spank of many!

Obviously no one remembers too much of their first few years, although I think I recall the way Mum would help send me off to sleep as a baby. Lying in my cot, I wouldn't close my eyes unless my little hand could hold onto her finger, which may explain why I do find it so hard to sleep in bed alone these days!

This hand-holding story might give you the impression I was an insecure child but the opposite was true. When I was three Mum enrolled me at the nearby Wellow House School, a small prep school that is slap bang in the middle of twenty acres of parkland and playing fields – all very muddy and English. According to Mum, I was the kind of child who was inquisitive and easy-going, and enjoyed being around other children, so the first day ran pretty smoothly. In fact, I already had a friend there, Michael MacDonald, son of my godparents Kevin and Donna.

School days seemed to consist mostly of drawing and I remember one time the teacher asked us to draw what we wanted to be when we grew up. Many of the kids picked obvious things like doctors or astronauts, but even from an early age I was intent on becoming an artist, so that's what I drew – it seems like Spenny and Mum's love of art had found its way down to me.

When not in class, we'd be playing outside. There was a pond which seemed vast and mysterious and full of life, and I was particularly fascinated by the huge frogs and the way they would jump from lily pad to lily pad. Watching them hop around kept me entertained for hours, and from that young age I developed a love of wildlife and nature that has stayed with me. David Attenborough is a particular hero of mine. If I could have dinner with one person, it would probably be him. Pretty much the only things I watch on television nowadays are wildlife documentaries. You won't find me in a nightclub during Shark Week.

Growing up at Caunton was near enough perfect. Although Nina and my brothers were a lot older, they took time to hang out with their little brother. One of my favourite pastimes with James and Michael was go-karting. As mentioned, we had a track – The Band had made tarmacked roads around the grounds and linked them, so they worked on race days. We had about eight karts in the garages, so friends would come round and proper races would ensue. The smell of petrol can still take me back to those race days at Caunton and the exciting sight of the karts with their shiny bodies all lined up and ready to go. A love of cars and racing is in my family's blood . . .

Obviously I was a bit young to drive, so Mike and James would take turns to sit me on their lap and I'd laugh as we raced. They were both really good at it – Mike because he was handy at sports and competitive, and James because he was already racing in Formula Renault with Manor Motorsport. Dad was a partner in the company along with John Booth and race engineer Pete Sliwinski, both of whom have now gone on to Formula One and GP3. In 1994, James became both British and European Formula Renault Champion and along the way equalled Alain Prost's record of ten consecutive race victories – although James will never tell you about this or any of his other achievements, being the most modest, discreet person you will ever meet. Isn't it incredible how brothers and sisters can be opposites yet still love each other and get along and even live together as James and I have done for years.

Now and again we would also shoot rabbits, fish for trout, fly kites or collect conkers, and on clear, blue-skied days we would sit outside the village pub with juice for the kids and beer for the adults.

Although we had a comfortable life, our parents didn't spoil any of us. In particular, The Band believes that you will not value money, nor the things it provides, unless you earn most of it yourself and respect the system by only taking out what you put in. Unfortunately that has meant there have never been any large sums of money hitting our bank accounts! We children had to work for our pocket money by carrying out chores, like washing-up, sweeping the yards, working in the kitchen garden, cleaning and that kind of thing. Mum and Dad set a good example, being a practical pair who mostly ran the house themselves. We usually didn't have staff living in with us, although Monica and Violet, two ladies from the village, would come to help with the housekeeping. We did have a lovely chap who looked after the grounds – and still does – called Glenn Green. Wonderfully appropriate name, isn't it? Glenn lived nearby with his wife, Leigh, and their two daughters, Courtney and Jasmine, who were a little younger than me.

The girls and I would play together, which was great, but if you're intent on mischief, you need the company of boys too. My good mates, and partners in crime at the time, were Nicholas Heptonstall and Matthew Andrews – friends from school who were living nearby.

By the age of five we had discovered BB guns, and would head out onto the land to shoot pigeons. Often we surprised ourselves with beginners' luck, but that left us in a quandary when it came to disposing of the dead pigeons. Just what are you to do with them once you've shot them? One solution was to use the stiffening corpses to scare Matthew's older sister Emma. Unsurprisingly, she didn't like that sort of thing, which made it particularly interesting to hide a pigeon or two in places where she was bound to find them.

One day we hid a dead pigeon in a kitchen cabinet containing cutlery, knowing that Emma usually laid the table . . . Then, as if we were in a bad silent movie, we lurked in the kitchen, casually looking elsewhere. We laughed out loud when Emma produced the perfect horror-movie scream. I'm not sure if she's forgiven us, but I guess this is my opportunity to say sorry to Emma for the scares – but it was fun when I was six!

If I was a mischievous little tyke, I only had my parents to blame as Dad would sometimes tell me, smilingly, to 'be nice and naughty' when I went out to play somewhere. And what is a son to do but adhere to his father's wishes?

Don't imagine that I always got away scot-free though – far from it. Smaller misdemeanours might result in a raised eyebrow from Dad, or a slightly solemn shake of the head, but on very rare occasions really naughty behaviour would merit a spank. We called it 'a hiding' and, needless to say, I didn't like it. But then, who does?

There was one day, though, when Dad came to me and said, very seriously, 'Mike has been naughty. Do you think we should give him a hiding?'

Given that it was generally me who suffered these punishments, it seemed only fair that Mike should receive the same for once.

'Yes!' I said, puffing my chest out and marching into the laundry room, ready to watch.

Whack, whack, whack! Dad proceeded to give Mike a hiding, until I could take it no more and burst into tears. But then the two of them fell about laughing, and I gradually realized it was a practical joke and they had only been pretending by whacking the wall behind them. Dad and Mike said it was done firstly to joke with me, but also to show how important it was for brothers to pull together.

I never requested either of my brothers get a hiding again, and we have been very close for all of our lives.

Some of my happiest childhood memories are from our time at Caunton Manor. Even though I haven't been back for many years, I'd love to buy it myself one day. It would be the perfect home in which to bring up children . . .

CHAPTER 2

Vive la France

It must have come as a relief to Emma – and the pigeons – when Mum and Dad decided to relocate the family to a new base in Paris in order to live a different life. At six years old this was to be an adventure and I was happy to up sticks. Caunton Manor was put up for sale, and Mum, Dad and I moved into a rented apartment on the Île St-Louis in the middle of the river Seine, next to Notre-Dame Cathedral and bang in the centre of one of the most beautiful cities on earth, Paris.

For some reason, the main thing I remember about our stay is that close by the apartment was a delightful little patisserie which sold the tastiest home-made pastries imaginable. In fact, it was probably this establishment that is to blame for the fact I became a good bit chubbier than I should have been. Even today, thinking about that patisserie, my head is full of images of chocolate eclairs, tartes aux framboises, and those colourful little macaroons.

Nearly every day, The Band would go running along the

banks of the Seine, and then we'd head off on family outings to places like the Louvre and the Tuileries, and the Musée d'Orsay. Mum bought me a stylish French beret so I'd fit right in. The family used to laugh when it was hoisted onto my head, although I can't imagine why . . .

The elegance of Paris might be responsible for a strange foible I developed at that time – the inability to wear clothes with a pattern or a logo. I remember Mum having to sew a patch of cloth over the horse logo on a Ralph Lauren shirt before she could persuade me to put it on. Thankfully, living in Chelsea, the home of the checked shirt, has been a kind of aversion therapy and I'm almost over it. Though I had a setback recently when I spent the day filming *Made in Chelsea* within eyeshot of one of Proudlock's choicest patterned wife-beaters . . .

While I coped with leaving my mates back in the UK, it was more disappointing that Michael and James didn't move with us, but they were doing their own thing. Mike was seventeen or eighteen at the time and was finishing sixth form at Uppingham School. James was motor racing in Formula Renault, or F3, and in his spare time was a trainee derivatives trader in London. I missed them a great deal but we would speak on the phone and they would come to visit the Paris apartment, and we'd go back to London to visit them too. Meanwhile, Nina had met a lovely guy named Adam Mackie. They married, set up home in Italy, and today have four brilliant children and are busy living happily ever after!

My French was non-existent when we arrived in Paris,

but I was lucky that the teachers at my new school were supportive and helpful. It was a Montessori, an interesting little place that welcomed children from many nationalities. As a Montessori school, it had an unstructured approach. The pupils didn't have a desk or a chair, but would sit around in the classroom busying themselves playing with toys, looking at picture books or drawing on walls. I had never been one for paying attention to what was going on in school, so this freestyle approach had a lot of appeal.

One of the things I loved most about Montessori was that every Wednesday afternoon we'd be walked through the city as a group. The buildings were fascinating, with the zinc and lead cladding on the Mansard roofs so different to anything I'd seen in England. We visited the Musée d'Orsay, Champs-Élysées, Sacré Coeur Basilica, the wonderful glass structures of Le Grand Palais and Le Petit Palais, Les Halles, the Ritz, Hôtel Le Bristol, Hôtel Place de Crillon, the Jardins des Plantes and le Jardin du Luxembourg . . .

The little shops lining the Parisian side streets seemed full of treasures. I was a particularly loyal customer of an establishment selling semi-precious stones; the incredible variety of colours was mesmerizing. Mum would give me some money to invest in a gem and I would come back with a new crystal every week to add to my growing collection.

When the folks told me we were going on a family holiday to the Caribbean I was intrigued. With a nose for adventure, I found the prospect of discovering another new place very exciting. None of us knew then how important one of the islands would become to our family.

We were guests of my other godparents and now dear friends, Alex Lees-Buckley and his lovely French wife Françoise and their son Gaston, on the yacht *Parsifal.* We set sail from Antigua to Barbuda and then across to St Barths. The heat and endless days of sunshine were a welcome change from European weather, and I couldn't help wondering aloud why it wasn't as glorious as this back home all the time. Mum gave a wry smile at that one. I loved the ocean, loved hearing the waves seemingly kiss us as we floated along and enjoyed the movement of the yacht in the water. It was such a great new experience. Alex showed Gaston and me how to fish, and every now and then over the side we'd go, into the warm sea. He took us dinghy sailing and we had runs on jet skis.

Alex, who worked as a footman for the Duke of Northampton at Castle Ashby when he was a young man, is now the senior luxury big yacht broker for Camper and Nicholson. He has become a wonderful friend and has a special place in my life, and although we are a generation apart we laugh a lot, at exactly the same things. The Lees-Bees couldn't be more welcoming and kind as a family.

Back to the Caribbean, and after a few days the boat dropped its hook in the Bay of St Jean on the north side of St Barthelemy. Mum and Dad decided that we should spend a night or two at the old but legendary Eden Rock Hotel on St Barths, an island of about twelve miles square.

Eden Rock was the first hotel built on the island during the 1960s. Set on a wild and rocky outcrop of land, it had six wooden bedrooms at that time. Its construction was the project of Caribbean aviator and adventurer Rémy de Haenen, who had become mayor of St Barths, which at that time was administered by the island of Guadeloupe. I remember him as a thin man with a hawk-like face and bright eyes. Rémy bought the site in 1953, for two hundred dollars, from two old ladies – one of whom brought back one of his hundred-dollar bills the very next day. She said that Rémy had paid too much and the ladies were uncomfortable! The Band always liked that little tale.

Rémy built the various houses that made up the hotel when we first visited, partly with his own hands and partly with help from friends and the locals. At first, some of the islanders thought Rémy was quite mad in his venture, but perhaps he was something of a visionary who foresaw what would later come to pass: the success of high-end, low-volume tourism on this small but beautiful island. This was the way, he seemed to think, to establish a deeper level of prosperity for the five thousand people who lived there then.

Thanks to his intuition, Eden Rock and St Barths started to become *the* place to go for thoughtful celeb travellers who valued privacy, some of whom became his friends. In fact, Rémy viewed his visitors as more than customers, and whether they were famous or not, and wealthy or not, they were treated as friends and with generosity. Guests included Greta Garbo, with whom Rémy enjoyed a passionate affair, Howard Hughes, Robert Mitchum, the King of Sweden, as well as the admirable Rothschild and Rockefeller families, who bought land and built homes on St Barths which survive, rather stylishly, to this day. So a kind of arty, racy, high-end, sometimes naughty visitor group began to assemble – and, of course, they encouraged their friends to join them, forming the unique social mix and ethos which sets St Barths apart from the other Caribbean islands save, possibly, Mustique. So long as nobody was hurt, you could do pretty much anything you wanted. And that peaceful freedom continues to exist today.

When we checked into the hotel it was far from the splendid place it had been in Rémy's best years. Yet something of the special spirit and captivating beauty remained, so much so that the folks started to wonder . . . Life in St Barths was more colourful than life in Europe and, like Rémy, they could see that the island's unique circumstances made it an exciting place in which to invest.

Fortunately, the hotel had been put up for sale some time before – this was The Band's territory and he promptly swung into gear. Initially, the idea was to acquire Eden Rock and keep it as a family holiday home. But then there was a little bar running from the hotel, lots of interesting and attractive visitors, we were all open-minded, and the school down the road looked okay . . . And so Mum and Dad thought about the possibilities. The only thing that was clear was that it would take a lot of work to restore the place to its former glory. As it turned out, it would take twelve years of constant effort.

The purchase went through pretty quickly once we were back in Paris, and we planned to move to St Barths on 28 August 1995. I had turned seven about three weeks before we set off. The heavier stuff from Caunton and Paris was being sent by container, but Mum still managed to pack an incredible twenty-five big bags to take with us on the plane. Mum is not someone who travels light, although this time, to be fair, we were moving home. When we arrived at Charles De Gaulle airport, the check-in staff seemed to take a sharp intake of breath, and shaking their heads in disbelief, said, in that lovely French way, 'Ooh la la la la,' as the bags were popped one at a time onto the weighing machine. Several Air France personnel assembled to watch the overweight kilo counter spin to levels rarely witnessed before. Eventually, pricing negotiations were concluded and we were on our way across the Atlantic to our new home: Eden Rock, St Barths.

As soon as we landed, we were gripped by that great feeling you get when you start a new chapter in your life. Mum and Dad were ready for their latest adventure and said they were thrilled that I was with them and was going to be part of it. The only downside was that we would miss my brothers who had remained in the City to continue their careers as derivatives traders – sitting at adjacent desks – and Nina, who was busy with Adam and her family.

But drama was just around the corner. We had barely landed when we received news of an approaching hurricane. A phone call from Rémy confirmed it was going to be a big one. 'Be careful,' he said, 'it is dangerous.'

Mum and Dad's idea of a hurricane seemed to be along the lines that it was likely to be a bit windy for a while. Even so, The Band decided to begin working on the relatively old wooden buildings, assisted by his friend Steve Haines who, with his wife Lesley, had travelled out with us. They bolted shutters and reinforced roofs as much as possible. Local officials told islanders to head to the nearby concrete-built school for sanctuary, but Dad figured that the main house was built of stone and hardwood and should be about as strong as the school. So we stayed in our new home. There were no guests at this time, as we were taking over the property.

The work of storm-proofing continued for forty straight hours without rest or sleep for Steve and The Band. Then we waited for Hurricane Luis to arrive. We didn't wait long. Even at that young age, I felt as if a big experience was about to begin, and it turned out to be one of the greatest adventures of my life to date.

CHAPTER 3

HURRICANE LUIS

The radio was our best link with the other islands and the only source of information as events unfolded. From the radio we learned that Hurricane Luis was 1,200km in diameter and was moving across the sea at only 8kph, which was bad because it meant that the storm would be stronger. The slower the ground speed, the stronger the winds, which in this case were predicted to be gusting at over 250kph. Luis was to be the most powerful storm to hit the area in living memory.

On Monday 2 September the wind suddenly increased until it was screaming through every weak joint in the hotel's defences. We peeked outside and saw it yanking mightily at the coconut trees and the other buildings on the island. Then we heard the shutters from the north and west end of the roof blow away and the windows cave in. These areas had been reinforced just before we'd arrived, so The Band hadn't thought it was necessary to do any further work on them.

It was too rough to climb onto the roof to fix the shutters so the folks moved some of our more valuable bits of furniture to what they thought would be safer areas of the building. As the storm continued, we began to feel a sense of anticlimax. Aside from the damage to the shutters and windows, the wind and rough seas did not seem as terrible as the stern warnings from the radio had led us to expect.

Then, at 1 a.m. the next day, the radio announcer said that the hurricane was coming.

'The hurricane *is* coming,' Dad said mildly.

We couldn't believe it – if Luis still hadn't hit the island, what exactly were we experiencing now?

The radio announcer continued by describing the current weather as merely a tropical storm, but added that the eye of Luis was on a direct route to St Barths, and repeated his warning that anyone able to do so should immediately head to shelter. Finally, before ceasing transmission (to try to save his equipment, he said), he introduced the governor of the island who, rather chillingly, wished everyone luck and God's blessing and prayed we would survive this thing together.

There was a moment's silence while the adults gathered their thoughts.

'Ooh,' Mum said, 'the hurricane's arriving after lunch.'

Although I was too young to understand the severity of the situation, I could tell from the glances between the others, and from the tense atmosphere, that this was not going to be straightforward. One thing we did know: it was far too late for us to go to the local school for shelter, even if we'd wanted to. There was also no chance of going to bed while all this was happening as the folks felt it best if we all stuck together and stayed alert.

By two o'clock on Tuesday, Luis was close and the world around us had changed. It became impossible to distinguish between sea and sky; instead, there was just this grey mass of wind and water smashing and hammering all around. The noise can only be described as one of continuous explosions. The storm was mesmerizing and spectacular, but we were too concerned about the glass shattering inwards to look through the remaining windows. Dad and Steve would, however, creep outside from time to time to fix bolts through the window and door frames. Sometimes nature can create scenes that are both beautiful and deadly, and we sensed that the adventure unfolding would remain with us for the rest of our lives.

The Band didn't have time to enjoy the experience. With Luis attacking from the north, Dad wanted to reinforce the old windows and a door in the restaurant that faced that direction. Using the heavy hardwood tables in the restaurant, and our twenty-five bags of luggage which were still waiting to be unpacked, Dad and Steve built a table and luggage island up against the door and windows. The whole structure was sheeted together with tarpaulin and rope. Who could say if it would hold, but it was the best weight we had.

At around 3 p.m. on Tuesday, the hurricane consumed the island. Outside, millions of tons of seawater were rolling and racing across the shore, sweeping their way through beach-side restaurants and houses and taking with them anything that wasn't concreted down. Trees, roofing and other debris shot through the air, landed and bounced, crashing onwards and causing more damage.

Debris continued to hit the hotel with terrific force. The Band wondered if constant battering would weaken the building. We had lost the room under the roof with the old shutters so now, despite being some 100ft above the sea, seawater poured through the windows, the roof and into the house. At the same time, a series of seemingly endless, hammering blows continued to rock the structure to its foundations and beyond. Concrete columns began to twist and bend.

That was actually quite a scary moment. The adults had been doing their best to make the whole thing seem like a game for me, and I'd been fairly calm throughout, but with the seawater pouring in and the noise reaching a crescendo, I began to feel like Leo on the *Titanic*.

Dad questioned if the weakest north-facing door could last. Hunched together in the strong lee-side kitchen, we watched the door through apertures in the wall, expecting it to explode inwards. Surely it would go, and with it the ceiling and that roof too – and then our only option would be to crawl to the underground rainwater system, which had been drained as a final possible bolt-hole. At one point, Dad and Steve darted to the door and nailed an additional 8' x 4' timber sheet to the inside frame.

Steve and The Band suggested that this time Mum,

Lesley and I shelter under the strong concrete sink unit in the kitchen. I sat there with a kitchen bowl on my head – I'm not entirely sure how I thought that would help but I did it all the same. I was exhausted by this stage, but every time I started to doze off under the sink there would be another crash outside that would startle me into instant alertness.

By 5 p.m. the wind was starting to shift westwards, but the force was still as strong. Dad and Steve continued to fortify the house inside and out. It was a dangerous job and one that almost cost Steve his life. As he crawled outside to locate a coach bolt (which could be used to fix some shutters), he narrowly escaped being collected by the restaurant roof, complete with its external extractor fan assembly (weighing around 300kg), which was ripped off and flew past him, landing about fifty feet away. For the next fifteen hours, the two of them would occasionally just dash around the house to reinforce the windows and doors that had been ravaged by the winds with whatever materials could be found. Eventually, the upstairs beds were broken up and used for further reinforcements as we were running out of wood.

The radio revived briefly to give locals an update on what was happening. The news was not good: conditions on St Barths were described as 'un catastrophe' while the waves were described as 'énormes'.

As daylight faded, the house was wrecked, with salt water running freely through the ceilings and into the building. A large pelican appeared – a magnificent creature.

As he perched on the broken beds and chairs, he and I eyed each other with mutual interest; we were both taking shelter from the storm and looking for food. He needed a roof over his head and I shared some of our bread with him. For a moment I completely forgot about the hurricane. You don't find many pelicans in Paris.

Twenty hours later, as the third day came to an end, the pelican spread his wings and flew away onto a calming sea. His departure spelt the end of the storm, as Luis drifted away and headed north towards New York, where it hurled a 95ft wave at the *QE2*.

With the storm reduced to strong winds, the inhabitants of St Barths started to emerge to find scenes of devastation. Houses and hotels were wrecked and flung into the sea. Water and electricity systems were so badly damaged they were out of service for three weeks afterwards. Roads were blocked, and some parts of the island were almost unrecognizable. The bow section of a small boat was found 600ft up a hill in the centre of the island. On St Maarten, eight hundred boats were smashed and sunk inside the harbour, which had previously been regarded by yachties as a safe haven, a 'hurricane hole'.

Tragically, people lost their lives throughout the islands, and many thousands of animals were killed and the sea was poisoned. Shanty accommodation has no chance of withstanding the likes of Luis and many people were left homeless. In St Maarten, there were more deaths when gunfights broke out between looters and the Dutch police. But in St Barths, under a strong mayor, nothing similar happened. In fact, the community pulled together with the French army and navy forces, and everyone helped each other to clear up the wreckage.

My parents and Steve and Lesley came out of the storm with just a few cuts and bruises. Mum's habit of overpacking had worked in our favour. When we went to check the north door, the bags that had been piled up against it hadn't moved an inch. As The Band said, 'We were saved by the luggage.'

CHAPTER 4

Home to the Iguana

The month following Hurricane Luis was a busy one. Eden Rock had been badly damaged and Dad set to work straightaway, repairing and restoring the building structures with the help of a small, strong team. He also began to design some renovations and improvements – and as the project grew over the years, so his team evolved to include a number of local artisans. I remember my parents talking about the hotel and their plans to create a home-like ambience within each building. Even back then they were aiming to develop a world-class business – one that would allow guests to experience the rich, vibrant culture on offer in St Barths. They reasoned that St Barths was such a unique place that their hotel should be extra special to match it.

Mum focused on the interior design and worked hard to avoid the uniform look typically associated with luxury hotels. She decorated each space differently and used an unusual yet charming mix of furniture brought from

Caunton together with the original Breton, Norman and St Barthian pieces left behind by Rémy. Dad had said to Rémy when shaking hands on the deal, 'Please leave everything, including the junk, and take away only your toothbrush.' Rémy had laughed; he and Dad had similar natures.

At this time we were living wherever the building guys were working least, and so home and hotel became one. Having the restaurant and kitchen services adjacent certainly helped to reduce the work of preparing lunch and throwing dinner parties – and tidying up afterwards was a lot easier too. Over the years, the three of us continued to live in the renovated sections of the hotel, occasionally moving from one house to the next, which allowed Mum and Dad to pick up ideas on how to improve and refine the design of future builds. In all, twenty-three houses were constructed, plus two restaurants and bars and a couple of boutiques, gardens, pools, etc.

Hurricane Luis helped Dad to understand the integrity of local structures and how to strengthen them so they could withstand violent weather. He also learned how to make buildings that were open when the weather was beautiful but quick to close up when showers blew through – which in the tropics is quite often. This rapid opening/closing is achieved mainly with rolling sail-like covers that are manually wound up or down instead of being electrically powered, as salt and sun quickly spoil the motors.

Between 1996 and 1998, Mum used to mention *Fawlty Towers* quite a lot, but slowly things began to improve.

Over time Eden Rock, St Barths evolved from modest and broken beginnings to become a fixture in listings of the world's top 100 hotels, which is a testament to all of the Eden Rock team.

Outside Eden Rock, I was getting to grips with a way of life that was totally different from London and Paris. The language of St Barths is French and I felt pretty complacent at becoming the first Matthews to speak a foreign language. The island atmosphere was a lot more laid-back than I was used to; there were no traffic jams or impatient drivers beeping their car horns. It always seemed to be sunny, and there was a lot of wildlife, including hummingbirds in the sky, and turtles, tarpons, barracuda and brilliantly coloured reef fish in the sea. We missed Nina and my brothers but otherwise this new lifestyle suited us.

I was enrolled at L'École Primaire de Gustavia, one of three good state schools on the island. The structure of the school was a little more formal than in the UK, and certainly more structured than the Montessori in Paris, and the syllabus was full-on French. We studied geography, history, maths, French of course, and the newly introduced subject of English which, unsurprisingly, was my favourite. Speaking better English than the teachers was both a good thing and a bad thing; it helped me to become popular with my classmates but I was no doubt unpopular in the staffroom, as it was impossible to resist the temptation to correct the teachers. And it wasn't just in my English lessons that I enjoyed sharing my opinion . . . Once my geography teacher told us that the United States of America wouldn't have succeeded in becoming the economic superpower it is today if it wasn't for the French! Even then, aged seven, I knew that wasn't quite right. Looking back, the good metropolitan French staff must have occasionally been exasperated by this cheeky, tubby foreign kid.

Not that I was a bad or disruptive pupil, maybe just a little cocky at worst. The biggest problem was my attention span, which was, and still is, light-switch short. My mind is quickly distracted and I find it all too easy to drift away. I wasn't particularly academic and it wasn't in my nature to strive to achieve As, but if I knew I could get one easily, I'd do the work required.

I preferred one-to-one lessons with a private tutor, finding it much easier to learn that way. Mum and Dad understood that I could not sit down and revise of my own accord, but with a tutor for a week or two I did okay. In general, though, I was happy to settle for lower grades so I could have fun outside of school. That's all I wanted to do. Go out and play in the sun with my mates and experience this new world. It was like life at Caunton – full of freedom and adventure – and a wonderful way for a child to be brought up. I was very lucky.

Happily for a newcomer to these parts, I had lots of friends. It may have been because I was seen as an exotic foreigner, or because I remained a naturally chatty and sociable child, but my classmates let me into their lives pretty easily, for which I was grateful. My closest mate at this time was a guy called Clovis, a skinny French lad with blond hair. He was a speedy little thing, too, and ran around like a Yorkshire whippet. Unsurprisingly, his favourite game was British Bulldog, because he knew that nobody was ever close to catching him. We bonded on my first day at school and he and his family made me feel very welcome indeed. We hung out by the basketball court and would often eat lunch together at his dad's harbourside restaurant. Then we'd explore the beaches and the caves, or 'les grottes' as they are known, and the tide pools on the shoreline. We'd also stroll along the sand and pick up spiders and crabs and any other such wildlife. I took them back to the hotel and made a collection. Loving nature, I was intrigued by how these little creatures lived. Dad found himself having to keep an eye on the well-being of my very own private zoo. One evening he smiled, and Mum yelled in alarm, when a crab demonstrated their amazing ability to pincer a target and then shed that leg, leaving the pincer biting tight – in this case, onto my thumb. Fifteen love to the crab.

We also befriended an iguana who lived around the hotel. Hercule, as we called him, was the most fantastical creature, being armour-plated in a prehistoric way and massive, slow and strong – and either dumb or brave, it was difficult to tell. If iguanas were fifty times bigger, they would rule the world. Hercule did exactly as he pleased. If he wanted to lie in the sunshine in the road, he would do, no matter how much a car driver might be hooting at him to get out of the way. Hercule had very little concern for the authority of others – a bit like Grandpa Spencer, come to think of it – and everyone loved him too. Hercule was a major hit with many of the guests, who would have their picture taken alongside him; others were less fond.

I would feed Hercule bread, and pour ice-cold water on his back, which he loved. He would arch his back and point his nose to the sky, graciously allowing me to attempt to get in his good books. He was a regal creature. Dad did murmur one day that he ought to find a way to monetize Hercule.

Then something happened to turn my seven-year-old mind away from boys' games. In a flash, thoughts usually filled with where to swim next and what I should feed Hercule were taken over by a girl . . .

Out on the beach and playing one day, I saw a little girl with lovely curly black hair and knew instantly that I wanted her to be my best friend. Heading over to talk, I found out she was called Meryl, was from Buffalo in Texas, and was staying with her parents nearby.

During Meryl's stay we grew to really like each other and I tried to be the proper little charmer. I took her to the one magic show St Barths had to offer and we dined at the finest restaurants (at least in the opinion of seven-year-olds) with our parents, who had also become friendly. Meryl and I were inseparable. Even at this young age I was most definitely a wannabe romancer. I knew instinctively that I had to take Meryl to all the right places: the magic show, the shops where you could buy the best sweets, the perfect spot to build sandcastles – even James and Mike were roped in to help, as they were both visiting at the time.

I don't think we kissed. The most we did was cuddle and hold hands while we walked along the beach. Sadly, our mini romance was brought to a sudden close when Meryl and her family headed back to Texas. I felt sad that our magical time had to come to an end. Without Meryl to hang out with, life would be pretty blue. I asked Meryl's parents to let her stay in St Barths just a few days longer. But, tragically, my pleas fell on deaf ears and Meryl went home, leaving me feeling alone and maybe just a little bit lovelorn.

So what is a seven-year-old boy to do when his first love has been taken away? Write a letter, of course – with the help of two older and more experienced brothers! It was important that the letter was perfect. We spent ages discussing it, trying to find the right words to express how much I missed her. I insisted that the letter should fit on just one side of paper, almost like a piece of artwork. I didn't want anything to be out of sight. It had to be frameable. I was extremely particular and told Meryl that she was very nice, that she had stood out from the crowd and that I looked forward to seeing her again. It was a love letter written from a seven-year-old heart – and using a felt-tip pen. I decided the letter must be written in the perfect colour, and although there were only six to choose from at the shop, it took me ages to select the right one. In the end I went with a passionate red.

I duly sent this letter to Meryl in Texas and she wrote back . . . and that was it.

Surprisingly, the pain wasn't as bad as I'd thought it would be and anyway I was easily distracted as usual, hanging out with my boys on the beach and playing with the collection of Action Men I had been accumulating every birthday. Memories of young, beautiful Meryl with the curly black hair, who had so mesmerized me for that blissful week, began to fade. A characteristic of mine that still impedes to this day – and maybe beyond?

In retrospect, perhaps our lack of contact was something of a blessing because Meryl returned to the island some years later – and by then she was a foot and a half taller than me. When we saw each other we felt completely different and the moment had passed. Our summer romance was just a particularly fond memory.

Hopefully Meryl is happy and prospering, and if you read this, my beautiful curly-haired friend, please tweet to say hi.

CHAPTER 5

Spencer – Gambling Account

I can remember the exact date my innocence was tarnished forever. It was 25 December 1996, and I was eight years old.

It was our second Christmas in St Barths. Our Christmases there were like anyone else's in Europe – apart from the sunshine. We exchanged presents and ate turkey with cranberry sauce. Before I went to bed on Christmas Eve, my parents, like any others, would place a glass of brandy and a slice of cake for Father Christmas underneath the tree. This year I'd insisted that Santa preferred milk and biscuits after a hard night of present-delivering, but Dad maintained otherwise and who was I to argue with adult wisdom? I shrugged and went to bed, excited by the knowledge that Santa would be paying us a visit that night and feeling confident he'd be leaving behind goodies in large numbers.

Rushing to the tree very, very early the next morning, I was brought up short when I bumped into the Band swigging the brandy.

'Hang on, Dad, that's for Santa,' I objected. At the same time, my inner detective was kicking into action. Dad's insistence on brandy and cake now looked strange. If we were really leaving it out for him to guzzle, did that mean . . .

'Er, thing is . . .' Dad said blankly. He was probably trying to decide how much he could get away with, but realizing that his son was putting two and two together, he came clean. It was a significant moment of course, as it is for all of us, but I took it pretty well. It didn't spoil Christmas for me and, since then and to this day, the Matthews family Christmas in St Barths is always a date in our calendar and the family, and some friends, make the effort to be there too. It's our chance to catch up and be together and we have a great time.

I always loved it when Nina and the brothers came out to visit. Mike and I were identical growing up, despite the fact he was twelve years older. If you were to look at pictures of him as a kid and of me at the same age, you'd get us mixed up. Even Mum says she still finds it hard to tell us apart in photographs. It's odd how similar we actually were, more so than James and I. It was as if we were connected in a deeper way than the usual brotherly bond, like twins separated by time.

That's not to say that I didn't get on with James. On the contrary, James was, and is, my strength and special friend. But growing up he was the sensible brother, while Michael and I were the mischievous ones. James was so different from the two of us. His career in motor racing really took off. James had won seventeen out of twenty-two races and two championships in 1994. There was talk of him maybe making it to Formula One, but being James, he'd looked at the percentage chances of success and cleverly decided to leave racing and instead become a trader in the City full-time.

Maybe because he had had this early career in high-level sport, James matured faster than your typical young man and possessed values that a child like me didn't understand or even recognize at the time.

So it was up to Mike and me to keep the Matthews household buzzing; not that Mike didn't have a hard-working, sensible side too – he did – he just tended to forget it when we were together. Sometimes, Michael would jump on James and tie him up so that I could tickle him, or pin him down while I drew on his face, and we'd all end up laughing hysterically. James and I would play-fight all the time and it was always Mike who would facilitate my win. It wouldn't have been possible without him. On rare occasions we fought as brothers do, but on the whole, James, Mike and I were The Three Musketeers.

As a boy, I wanted Nina's heart of gold, Mike's general character and James's girlfriends. Although both my brothers had good taste in women, James was always the pickiest of the two. He had some absolutely incredible girlfriends.

My own awareness of the opposite sex was about to shift from being innocently attracted to my brothers' dates to a deeper understanding of what went on between men and women – courtesy of Mr Bruce Willis. I've always watched movies with a much higher rating than my age, partly because I had older brothers and found the movies they hid, and so was familiar with his work in the *Die Hard* films. But *Color of Night* was something different . . . Let's just say Brucey opened my eyes somewhat.

Movie night took place in Spencer's Cabin – as my room at Eden Rock was then, and still is, called – and the audience consisted of Arthur and Alex Cohen, who were twins two years above me at school, et moi. They were fun guys and we hung out a lot. The movie had a bit of a reputation because it featured a sex scene that was supposedly pretty explicit so, needless to say, we were well pleased when we eventually got hold of the DVD. I've forgotten most of the plot, but the scene where Bruce makes love to a rather attractive woman in the pool, then the shower, then the bedroom, are moments I will remember forever. There was full-frontal Brucey nudity and it was the first time I had ever actually seen sex and got a clear idea of what it was. It did hold one's interest. That night, lying in bed on my own, I replayed the scenes in my mind and became more acquainted with my own body and the sensations it was capable of feeling. A whole other world had been opened up to me, and I was keen for the day to arrive when I could follow the lead of Mr Willis.

I soon discovered that it wasn't going to be as easy as had been hoped, what with only being eight years old at the time. Fortunately it wasn't long before we stumbled across some altogether more educational material. Clovis and I were round a friend's house one afternoon, and this friend happened to have an older brother whose room was out of bounds. Kids never like hearing that things are out of bounds so naturally we took to searching it for any sort of contraband we could find. Hidden away in the back of a wardrobe was a stack of interesting DVDs . . . We never watched *Color of Night* again.

We sat down to watch the DVDs together and the experience was certainly enjoyable, yet shocking. This was full-on; it was a whole new world and we quite liked it. It was fascinating at the time and knowing that we were too young to watch this kind of film made it all the more exciting.

When we weren't on the beach, Clovis, Alex, Arthur and I would spend much of our spare time playing *Mario Kart* and *Goldeneye* on our Nintendo 64s. That kept us busy – but only for so long. I found it very easy to gain access to the keys for one of the restaurants, where we knew we could find lots of treats for boys with a hunger for sweet things. So occasionally, when the staff had closed up and left, we would sneak into the empty restaurant, hunt out the chocolate tarts made for the following lunch service, and scoff the lot. Next day, the guests would order tart and the staff would be puzzled when they couldn't find any. My expanding waistline was to be the largest clue. But it was worth it as those tarts were as delicious as the pastries in Paris had been.

When we weren't wandering around the island committing minor crimes, the boys and I formed a basketball team which we called Le Fox. We'd practise for hours on end, trying to shoot hoops. Why we did it, who can say, as we had no rival team to actually take on, but we enjoyed the camaraderie – and the exercise counteracted the stolen tarts which was a bonus.

Although my social life was busy, there was time to nurture my artistic side, and I was forever drawing and painting. My strongest skill was copying other pictures without tracing. I'd only have to look for a few moments to be able to replicate an almost exact copy on a fresh piece of paper. Definitely a touch of Grandpa Spencer in there.

At the same time, I was beginning to understand the value of money and had realized that if I had my own cash I could pretty much buy what I wanted – which at this point in time meant computer games, DVDs, sweets and Action Men. So I hit upon the idea of using my artistic skills profitably to create limited edition picture cards for the guests at Eden Rock to buy. I'd draw parrots, Marilyn Monroe, seascapes, St Barthian landscapes . . . whatever came to mind. Each year the subject was different, and the artwork was signed and dated. Even at eight or nine, my art was not too bad, even if I say so myself, and my parents still keep bits of work I produced all those years ago.

The guests loved the cards. The Americans, as usual, were the most generous, handing over seven dollars for each one just like that, so I would always make a beeline for them. Over the years, I've come to realize that Americans often are the warmest people on the face of the earth. Outside of the Christmas period, I'd also sketch guests at the bar and try to flog the pictures to them.

When my artwork had made around a hundred dollars, I'd ask The Band to exchange the money for single dollar bills. I felt triumphant with that impressive wad of money in my hand, as though I were a successful businessman. And while the folks were amused by the mini business venture, I think they were also proud of my enterprising spirit.

Unfortunately not everyone was as kind or generous to a young artist as the guests on St Barths. On a trip back to Paris, one time on the Eurostar, I decided to whip up a few drawings to sell to the other passengers. Clutching my pieces of art, I walked up and down the aisle trying to make a few bob. But no matter how hard I tried, the French and the Brits just weren't biting. Instead of buying, they'd smile and laugh and not purchase a single thing. I went back to my seat feeling despondent, thinking, *Not so easy but let's keep trying.*

As you may have gathered, I was confident and rarely fazed, and would entertain myself befriending hotel guests. I was always polite – with The Band's often repeated phrase of 'Manners maketh man' ringing in my ears. One lady even wrote a letter to my parents after leaving the hotel, saying, 'What an unusual little boy . . .' Not quite sure what she meant by that.

Dad encouraged me to work as a waiter, serving lobster to the customers on the beach (lobster was caught in surprising numbers around St Barths and was a speciality at Eden Rock).

'I work here,' I would explain reassuringly to customers who didn't know me – just in case they thought I was a waif and stray who had wandered up. Generally, they thought it was worth a smile. The other waiters didn't much like it though, as I was sometimes tipped a bit more for the novelty of being served by such a young boy.

By now we'd been living in St Barths for about three years and Mum and Dad had transformed the buildings and increased the scale of the operation. Celebrities were visiting, just as they had for Rémy. One visitor who made my tenth birthday particularly exciting was Mariah Carey. She rocked up to the hotel looking beautiful, all long brown hair, tanned skin and curves. She was really nice and was not at all the diva that she is sometimes portrayed as being. Best of all, as soon as she found out it was my birthday, she insisted on giving me a birthday kiss. It was only on my cheek, mind you, but there was certainly no objection.

Just as memorable were encounters with the mighty rapper P Diddy, or Puffy as he was known back then, a name Dad still insists on calling him today. Puffy ended up visiting St Barths a few years in a row and was the most charming of guests. Sure, he was a famous guy with a fortune, but at Eden Rock he was able to kick back and relax. So whenever I would trot up to him he was always very friendly, asking how I was and really taking an interest in what I had to say.

I remember one particular day when he was relaxing on the beach with Jennifer Lopez, who he was dating at the time. He loved his lobster, and after I had taken it down to him we ended up chatting as usual, and that led to him teaching me how to play backgammon, which has since become a bit of a staple hobby of mine. The whole celebrity thing didn't faze me – and still doesn't. He was approachable and, best of all, I managed to beat him at backgammon. Although he may have given me an edge . . .

Later, I became quite good at the game, having mastered the rules and the variety of opening rolls and winning combinations as well as learning how to read people's faces. This was all thanks to an old mate Michael Davies, an architect from New York who regularly stays at Eden Rock and became *the* backgammon guru, teaching me how to play properly. He was so good he played pro tournaments, but that didn't mean I couldn't beat him. I am proud of these victories – he less so! Fortunately, backgammon has rather a large element of luck to the game – something I've never been short of.

And so I began making money. The Band set me up with an account at the local bank in Gustavia, which he called 'Spencer – Gambling Account'. It was a brilliant idea. At one point, I had about $1,200 in winnings from working, selling sketches and playing backgammon games on the beach. I felt like I'd made it.

CHAPTER 6

Michael

Swimming towards the jump spot had been bad enough. Now, stepping up to the cliff edge, the discomfort had fully settled in. Fifty feet below, the swirling waves were crashing over what appeared to be jagged rocks. I was paralysed by fear, but however impossible it seemed, I had to jump. It is not in my nature to do 90 per cent of the work and not finish the job. I was out for the day with a group of boisterous young French lads a few years ahead at school, who had decided to go cliff-jumping. I had not made it a commonly known fact that heights were not my thing.

One by one, the other boys leapt off the edge of the cliff. In a way it looked thrilling and liberating and their enthusiastic shouts as they plunged, seemingly in slow motion, towards the ocean below suggested it was a lot of fun, but now it was my turn and it was a different story. My feet seemed glued to the rock. It is often the case that the longer one leaves these moments the harder the task in hand becomes – like when jumping out of a plane for instance. Stepping forward, balancing on the edge, my heart rate began to increase. Deciding it was now or never, I threw myself off the top of the rock. My eyes were tightly shut for what seemed like minutes but in reality it was all over in a heartbeat. Reaching the surface of the water, I felt triumphant and had a huge grin on my face. My fear of heights, while perhaps not conquered, had at least been confronted.

A sense of adventure and thrill-seeking is one of the Matthews family traits. That was most true of my brother Mike. He really was a mix of James and me, sharing my general love of life but also possessing James's work ethic and something of his more serious side. In many ways, he was the most rounded member of the family.

Michael was the sort of person who had difficulty sitting still. He loved the idea of travelling the world. His gap year after Uppingham was spent moving around Africa, his time away seeming to consist of high-intensity sports such as bungee jumping, sky-diving, exploring and falling asleep on bar stools. Mike had an attractive character and whoever he met recognized this. He made friends all over the globe, some of whom remain close to our family to this day. Mike was a firm believer that you have one life and that it is not to be wasted.

Climbing was his main passion and he was always striving towards breaking boundaries. During his time at Uppingham, he'd climbed in Wales, the Swiss Alps, the

Pyrenees and Kilimanjaro in Tanzania. He was an experienced climber, fast and strong. The thought of climbing the world's highest peak would have crossed my brother's mind but it took an article he read on a slow day at work to persuade him to make the move. He began to test the water by talking to a friend, Jamie Everett. Jamie was keen. The lads knew that Everest was dangerous but this did not slow them down.

The magazine article mentioned a company called Out There Trekking (OTT) which organized trips to Everest, and Mike got hold of the company's brochure. He was persuaded even though the price of a place on the expedition was $40,000. But that price included everything, such as the latest equipment, and Michael had done well as a trader and could afford it. His mind was made up. He invited Dad to join him and Jamie on the Everest climb, and the three of them went on training expeditions in the French Alps, followed by Mount Aconcagua in Argentina, all with OTT. The trips went well, apart from the fact that Dad was forced to withdraw as he had problems at altitude as a result of the injuries he'd suffered in the car crash at Silverstone. It would be just Mike and Jamie making the attempt on Everest.

Mum, Dad and I were back in the UK and staying in London's Grosvenor House Hotel to see Mike off. The family spent a pretty ordinary day together, just chatting and reading the newspapers. There was no big deal about Mike heading off on this particular adventure – it was just what he did. I thought to myself that I was looking forward to his return.

He kissed me on the forehead before he gave us all one of his mischievous grins and headed to the airport, rucksack on his back. It would be the last time I ever saw him for Michael was to die on Everest. His loss was devastating for the family, and over time this became worse because the circumstances surrounding Michael's death have never been fully explained. Following years of detailed research, Dad is finalizing a book in which he shines light on some of the less well-known and worrying aspects of the Everest mountaineering 'industry'. I will leave it to him to provide the full detail when he publishes. In the meantime, here is an outline of what happened to Mike.

Mike and Jamie departed for Nepal on 21 March 1999. Having arrived, Mike and the other OTT expedition members divided into small teams for the long walk to Everest Base Camp, where they arrived on 6 April, having acclimatized to the high mountains to some extent along the way. However, after ten days at Base Camp, Jamie suffered altitude sickness and had no alternative but to return home early to the UK.

OTT's Director, Jon Tinker, was the leader of the expedition. Mike was placed in a group with three other paying clients – Canadians Denis Brown and Dave Rodney, and Yorkshireman Chris Brown. It was a big expedition, and the clients were to be supported by guides and sherpas.

After a series of preparatory climbs between Everest Base Camp and Camps 1, 2 and 3, around 3 May the group finally reached Camp 4, the highest camp, where they intended to rest for the night before making a summit attempt. But before the final push could be attempted, John Tinker informed the group that he was ill and the whole team returned with him back down the mountain. Keen to have pressed on, Mike was not happy about this.

But Tinker's descent from Camp 4 was not just to Base Camp. Leaving the expedition in the hands of a senior guide, Nick Kekus, Tinker returned to the UK where his wife had given birth to their first baby days earlier. A week later, and without its original leader, the team went for a second attempt.

On 12 May my brother finally arrived at the summit. We will never know how he felt but I reckon he would have been content. As Dad always stated, Mike did not climb for accolades, he just climbed. But his progress to the summit had been very different from his climbing since he had arrived in the Himalayas. The other clients told us that, until summit day, Mike had usually been right at the front, climbing swiftly and strongly. On summit day, though, he appeared to be struggling, and was almost the last of the group to reach the top.

After twenty minutes or so at the top, Mike and Mike Smith, an OTT guide who arrived near the summit at the same time, started their descent together on the fixed ropes, which sherpas install each year for the Everest climbing season. As they descended, the weather changed, turning ferocious with a snowstorm whipped up by 100 mph winds. Smith recalled later that Mike was joking at the summit and was conscious and lucid on the descent, making his way down from the summit slowly but surely. But as the conditions worsened and the weather closed in Smith and Mike became separated leaving Mike alone and the last man on the mountain.

Smith's evidence was that he stopped lower down and waited for Mike to appear. But it was too late. Mike did not appear. Smith headed back to camp alone.

While Mike was away in Nepal, we went back to St Barths and life for me continued as usual. I was gallivanting around the resort with my French mates and Mum and Dad were working in the business.

One night I was in my bedroom, Spencer's Cabin, when I got a call to go upstairs to see my parents. I couldn't think of anything naughty I'd done recently.

Mum and Dad were alone and looking very strange indeed. Mum looked like she had been crying and Dad too – this had never happened before in our family, and it hasn't happened since. My heart started thumping as something was obviously very wrong.

Dad told me that a storm had struck Everest while Mike was climbing, and that Mike was missing on the mountain. I heard the words but didn't really understand their significance. In my heart I believed that Mike would be found – or make his way home – and would come bursting through the door at any minute with his big smile. It took days for the truth to settle in. Having had no experience of loss, it was unfamiliar territory for a ten-year-old mind and in many ways I'm happy I was that age as the reality didn't sink in until much later in life. I genuinely believed that Mike would just walk back into our lives again. It was simply impossible for me to come to grips with the thought that I'd be separated from my brother for ever.

When my parents confirmed that Michael was lost to us I still didn't really believe it. But in the end I had no choice other than to begin to come to terms with the fact that he was gone. I would never see my beloved brother again, never see his face or spend any adult time with him. It was devastating.

My parents always remained strong. They didn't weep in front of us, but to this day their eyes may water a little when Mike's name is spoken during a conversation.

James of course took the news badly. With just a year and a half between them, he and Mike were the closest of friends. The loss was heartbreaking for James. Now, at the age of twenty-five, I have a better insight into how he must have felt. If anything were to happen to James, I can't imagine how I would cope without his strength. He is there for me through thick and thin, in his private, modest and calm way.

On Mike's birthday, we send Mum and Dad red roses for the age he would have been. I guess that our family's way of dealing with losing Mike is to believe that he goes on with us. It's just that he's in another place.

Dad wrote to *The Times* and thanked OTT and its guides for their efforts on the mountain. Although Mike's death was widely reported and although the letter in *The Times* carried our address, none of the mountaineering authorities attempted to contact the family. My parents were on their own, which was fair enough. They began by hoping that Mike's body could be recovered from Everest, although they were very clear that they never ever wanted anyone else's life to be put in danger in the attempt. It was troubling for them to think of the indignities that happen to the bodies of climbers left on the mountain, some of whom have been photographed as if they are just part of the scenery. There were stories of climbers being found frozen to ropes who are cut off and cast aside, or allowed to fall, by fresh expeditions going to the mountain at the start of each season. A Swedish expedition kindly offered to look out for Mike on the way up, and when they didn't find him we assumed he had been blown off the ridge and down the north-east face of the mountain, where at least he would have a private resting place. I've always found it comforting that Mike rests on top of the world.

Because Mike's body was never recovered, we have not been able to say goodbye in person. We have nowhere to go to so we can sit with him. So he lives on with us in our minds only.

A memorial service was held five months later at the lovely Grosvenor Chapel on South Audley Street in Mayfair. It was an emotional affair, of course, but there was laughter and optimism too. In his twenty-two years Mike had made tons of lively, amusing and admirable friends and about four hundred of them crammed themselves into the small church to say goodbye.

The day is hard for me to look back on, as there were so many emotions swirling around in my head. I remember that Mike's old headmaster, Stephen Winkley, gave an address and I was called upon to do a short reading from 'The Narrow Sea' by Robert Graves. I was nervous on the day, anxious not to let down my parents, Nina, James or the memory of Mike. The reading went well.

The headmaster of my school in London at the time, Mr Christopher Trevor-Roberts, was also present at the service and was kind enough to offer me a St Christopher's medal. I keep this safely.

Dad has continued to try to understand what happened to Mike, as sometime before the memorial service, he was called by someone who had been part of Mike's expedition. The caller told him about the climb and outlined some of the issues climbers faced as Everest expeditions became more commercialized. The caller was convinced that we did not know everything about Mike's time on Everest. Dad listened and reflected for a few days on what he had been told. He wanted to try and understand how and why Mike had died.

He made contact with some of the guides and clients who had been on the expedition and over the next few years he increased his effort. He worked mostly alone to collect written statements and other evidence. He always stayed calm and fair. I don't think I could have done that. He simply wanted to get to the truth and hoped to do so by talking to everyone. Some people refused to talk, and we felt the guiding community circled the wagons in order to protect itself. In January 2000, for instance, the British Association of Mountain Guides apparently met in a pub in Derbyshire to discuss Michael's death, and the role of its members. The family knew nothing about the meeting beforehand and was not invited to attend. The first my parents knew about it was when they were sent a copy of the meeting's findings, which totally exonerated their members. I know Dad feels that at the very least we should have been invited to see the process unfold.

But Dad was not the only one looking into the expedition. The *Mail on Sunday* and the *Sunday Times* both ran major investigative articles, from which the family learned a great deal.

We learned, for instance, of the role in the expedition played by a controversial character called Henry Todd. We found out that Todd had served seven years in prison after being convicted of being one of the leading figures in the LSD manufacturing ring exposed by Operation Julie in the 1970s. Todd had supplied the oxygen equipment to Mike and the group for their summit attempt. I know Dad was shocked that such a maverick had been working with Mike's team. Dad continued to look carefully at everyone involved.

Much was to happen over the following years, all of which

will be reported in detail in Dad's book. Almost all of it raised serious questions about the way climbing the world's tallest mountain has become commercialized. Dad believes that we are still in the dark over what really happened to Mike and how he came to lose his life, and that he owes it to Mike to try to get to the bottom of it. The process of fact-finding, which he began all those years ago, is what he is bringing together, finally, in his book. I can't wait to read it.

The family set up the Michael Matthews Foundation in his memory, of which James and I are trustees. It raises funds to help provide school buildings to children around the world who otherwise wouldn't receive an education. Mike would have supported this wholeheartedly and the charity ensures that his name is not left on the mountain, but lives on in our real lives. It is very much a family initiative with, for example, our cousin Luke Daynes who contributed to the fund again in 2012 when he and twenty-five of Mike's mates walked 50km in the London Thames Path Challenge. Mum's sister Pamela does great work too and so do Adam, Nina and their family.

But the individual who deserves most credit is James, who over the years has been tireless in his fundraising, taking part in countless marathons, triathlons and iron-man races in order to raise money. For example, in 2008, he completed the particularly gruelling Marathon des Sables which saw him run 245.3km over six days and nights through the Sahara Desert carrying more or less everything he needed for the entire trip. Also he came an impressive third place in the 2012 North Pole marathon. James is so selfless when it comes to his charity work for Mike's Foundation – he is a real stand-up guy. The world needs more men like my brother James.

CHAPTER 7

A Sudden Change

After Mike's death, Mum and I moved back to London for a while, staying at 39 Park Street in Mayfair, a house which belonged to Mike and James. Dad was living and working in Monaco, which was the family home. Mum and Dad had (and still do have) an apartment enjoying a fine view of the town. Monaco is very like St Barths in that both enjoy a peaceful, crime-free and full-on French way of life. This time it felt strange being in the UK. It was the first time we'd been back in England without Mike. I still half expected to see my brother pop up somewhere or give us a call to say he had been detained but was on his way back. As time passed, though, we adjusted as a family. And the return to normality meant I had to go back to school.

I had turned eleven when Mum enrolled me at the Trevor-Roberts Tutorial College in Swiss Cottage. She'd been thinking about temporarily moving back to England so that I could go to a British school even before the accident, because back in St Barths the senior school system was less well developed than the junior school.

Trevor-Roberts was small and accommodated around a hundred kids from the ages of five to thirteen. It prided itself on its academic success rate, which Mr Roberts reckoned was down to the small class sizes and the individual attention paid to pupils.

I have to admit I didn't really feel all that welcomed by the rest of the students when I started. I can't quite explain why, but I just didn't. They weren't exactly rude, but they didn't go out of their way to make new people feel welcome either. In fairness, they must have already formed their own circles of friends and here I was, this cocky tanned guy from the Caribbean, who could speak French as well as English, expecting to be accepted straightaway.

But over time I got to be part of the gang and became friends with chaps like Harry Hunt, James Both and Charlotte Porter. I don't know so much about Charlotte any more unfortunately, but James and Harry went on to be two pretty interesting individuals. Harry became a professional rally driver, something he always had a very good feel for growing up, and James was an excellent rugby player. I still bump into them fairly regularly in and about London.

Petra Ecclestone, daughter of Formula One boss Bernie Ecclestone, was also a classmate, and was really sweet and lovely. At that age, kids don't tend to understand the idea of family wealth, so she wasn't treated any differently from us – to us she was just Petra. She probably arrived at school in a Bentley with a driver, but a lot of classmates' parents had nice cars, and we would have just thought the chauffeur was her dad.

Dad once asked about her, though, probably because of his interest in racing. 'How is Petra? What's she up to? You should ask her out!'

It wasn't to be. It was a weird time for me, not only because we'd lost Mike, but also because London was so different from St Barths. The weather was an issue to deal with. I missed the constant heat and lightweight clothes I could wear back there. The way of life was very different too. In St Barths there was a more relaxed, fluid atmosphere. What happened happened – nothing was a big deal. But here at Trevor-Roberts, lessons and learning were more regimented than I was used to, which of course I found particularly difficult. I was also sad that at TRTC there was just a tiny playground and no sporting activity to speak of. I missed my old basketball court back in St Barths and the occasional practise sessions for matches that would never happen. I even missed the cliff-jumping. I was beginning to realize how great life had been in St Barths.

Eventually, I became acclimatized to the new surroundings and settled in, trying my hand at various extra-curricular activities, such as learning how to play the saxophone and acting. It was around this time that I became a bit of a thespian. I'd always loved movies, and was particularly into James Bond at the time. So while I was at Trevor-Roberts I took on several roles in school productions, including the lead in *Cyrano de Bergerac*, which I loved immensely. It was nice to be able to speak French in the UK as it was always a bit awkward being fluent during French lessons. This was not the time to look smug at the new school.

My time at Trevor-Roberts was the least exciting but most productive period of my life so far. They made us work so very hard that there was scarcely any time left for us to do or think about anything except homework and study, which meant I couldn't enjoy myself as I normally would. This was a school where learning and results mattered, and my usual end-of-year cramming technique didn't work here, as they put pressure on you to always be on top of things. So I was working pretty diligently the whole time I was there. Nightmare!

When Dad was visiting London, he would give me a better introduction to being English. We would visit various museums and historical buildings, such as St Paul's Cathedral and Apsley House by Hyde Park, where the Duke of Wellington lived. The Band loves history, especially the Duke of Wellington. We would have tea at one of London's hotels, such as The Ritz, Claridge's or The Connaught. It was good father–son stuff and entertaining, even though Dad seemed to enjoy it more than I did.

However, it was about my only release from school at that point as the folks had decided that they wanted me to try for Eton. To help me pass the common entrance exam, they asked my English teacher, Natasha Fogus, and Lucas

Pitts, who taught geography, to tutor me privately for a few weeks. This was when I worked best. One-on-one tuition meant that I wasn't so easily distracted and actually took in what I was listening to, no matter how dull it was at the time.

The exam was sat and I thought that I'd done okay although with the extremely high pass mark needed to get into Eton I could never have been certain. Back when I took the exam they were accepting one in seven pupils and I was hardly what you would call a good student – relying mainly on my interview in person with the lower master at the school. I felt like I had a good degree of life experience and honesty for a child of my age, something which The Band and I thought might differentiate me from other students. However, the grades had to be met and along came the morning when all of us in our final year of Trevor-Roberts were huddled in assembly awaiting our chosen college allocations – read out publicly. This was done in alphabetical order and when my name was not read out amongst the Ms an overwhelming sense of failure dawned on me. The end of the alphabet was reached and I felt harsh disappointment. All of the hard work I'd put in to try and make it into Eton had been completely wasted, but more importantly it felt as though I'd really let down my tutors and parents. I was just about to walk out of the room when Christopher Trevor-Roberts stepped back onto the stage and announced one final result.

'Oh yes, and Spencer Matthews . . . you got into Eton . . . just.'

I can't begin to explain the relief I felt, but I also couldn't help but develop a respectful hatred for Christopher, which lasted all of five minutes before I hugged him for the first and last time. He has since passed away but he was such a character and gave that school the excellent reputation that has since been upheld by his son Simon. If Trevor-Roberts can get me into Eton, it can achieve anything.

So I was off to Eton, an institution with an amazing history, which has schooled royalty, prime ministers and actors too, a few of my favourites being Dominic West, Damian Lewis and Eddie Redmayne.

In September 2000, when Mum and Dad drove me to what would be home for the next five years, I was surprisingly excited. As I've said, I welcome change and adventure, and what I'd taken from Mike's death was that every day is to be lived to the full. Well, to be honest, having just turned thirteen I probably didn't consciously think that, but I'm sure it influenced me then and that's definitely what I think now. Which is why I regret nothing. Regrets are a waste of energy; negative emotions that make life a whole lot messier than it needs to be. Things, good or bad, happen, and if you do something bad yourself, don't wallow in the agony of what you did; just learn from it and try to make sure you don't do it again.

I was revelling in having the opportunity to start a new chapter in a new school where, hopefully, academia was not the be all and end all. I'd heard such fantastic stories about Eton and what it can do for a young man and I was rather hoping there would be many interesting opportunities to come my way. I was looking forward to making great friends but was also excited about the lifestyle Eton promised. The sporting facilities were just outstanding and there were activities of many kinds to busy even the most active of students. There was a debating society which students were encouraged to join and I was particularly keen on pursuing my art and acting within the drama schools. Popular sports were, of course, available but of particular interest to me were the sports that Etonians had invented themselves. These were sidelines to the majors but interesting nonetheless. Two of these sports were the field game and the wall game, both physically demanding and usually played at the highest level by the top rugby players and footballers. The rules are a little too complicated to go into now but I highly advise catching a game. You could even go beagling – if you don't mind.

When we arrived at the 600-year-old school, it felt as if we were on a film set – it was like another world – huge spaces, high ceilings, interesting clothes and a high street full of shops. Once I was out of the car and walking around the buildings, I really appreciated just how large and impressive Eton was, and regardless of whether or not I liked the concept of school, I couldn't help but be moved and inspired by it.

The folks came with me to Walpole House, which was to be home. Like every new boy I had a study/room, containing a bed and a table. All I brought with me from home were pictures taken in St Barths and a photo of

Mike, James and Nina so that they were always with me. I've never needed much more than that.

It's possible Mum was having to fight back a tear as she hugged me goodbye, but I stayed cheerful. No sooner had I waved off my parents than some fresh-faced older boy came knocking on my door.

'Hello,' I said, wondering if I was about to make a new friend.

'Want to buy some porn?' he asked. 'It's a tenner.'

I knew there and then that my time at Eton was going to be fun.

CHAPTER 8

Attacking the Embassy

It didn't take long for me to settle into Walpole House with the fifty or so other boys, about ten of whom were also new boys. We were all in the same boat and keen to enjoy a bit of freedom and independence away from our families. Luckily, the lads I would be lodging with for the next five years seemed like a great bunch from our brief initial meetings and we all got on pretty well as the term progressed. Many of us are still friends today.

For those of you unaware of how the school works, here's a tiny bit about it. Each house has a housemaster who looks after and supports you. Our housemaster was the epic Mark Fielker, a very cool and understanding man. He was young for a housemaster and felt like a friend. Every housemaster has his own way of running his house, but Mark Fielker was – and still is – a top guy who looked after us without ever appearing to be that power-happy force that is so disliked by pupils at school.

The housemaster is assisted by a dame, who makes sure

that the boys' kit is in reasonable repair and that they are all tucked up in bed when they should be, and not out drinking. The dame is the one who has to deal with a couple of dozen somewhat questionable reports of sickness each morning. I'm not implying that the dame practised favouritism, but I certainly managed my fair share of sick days. We had two dames over the years, and I was particularly fond of Carolyn Turner. She was a pretty woman, a little bit like the matron in the *Carry On* films, and had a heart of gold.

Some of the senior boys had responsibilities, such as the house captain who would try to ensure that we enjoyed our time in the house and would encourage us to become fully involved in the activities on offer at the school. Then the captain of games would encourage us to play a range of sports, and would expect every boy to participate in house teams regularly. On arrival at the school I aspired to obtain this post. Team sport was something that I had looked forward to for some time since being accepted into Eton – a luxury that was not available at Trevor-Roberts Tutorial College. We were expected to choose one game each half to be our 'major sport'. In addition, we were given a brief taste, during our first two halves, of some of the 'minor sports' that Eton offers (chosen from a long list). In my first year I played rugby, hockey and tennis as my major sports, as well as cricket and soccer for the house. Throughout my time at Eton I experimented with all that was on offer, both on the sporting fields and the rowing lake, and with the societies.

Some of the houses enjoyed excellent breakfasts, lunches and suppers in Bekynton, a large central dining complex, while others – like my house – had in-house catering, which consisted of their own cooks and private dining rooms. Every house provided boys with time for mid-afternoon tea, which was an informal affair when we were able to make ourselves toast and things. This was called 'messing'.

As you'll know, the school is famous for its traditions, including a uniform of black tailcoat and waistcoat and pinstriped trousers. Whilst many kids aren't so keen to wear a uniform, Etonians as a rule understand the value of hundreds of years of tradition and wear the attire with pride.

People often ask about another old public school tradition, fagging, and whether it still exists at Eton, and the answer is no. Fagging was basically when an older lad got one of the younger boys to act like his servant and do all sorts of petty jobs. Before my time an example of fagging may have included warming the loo seat in the winter for someone who found the chill unwelcoming. I suppose it was a bit like bullying, but back then it was just part of the system. Unfortunately it is not possible to prevent all kinds of bullying nowadays and Eton no doubt has its fair share, just like any other school, but such is life and it's something that I can safely say I was never involved with. The ripping of ties is still fairly common at Eton and although this can't really be seen as bullying, it is a major inconvenience to have to go back to the house and change your tie, as of course without a tie you shall be punished.

These were, however, no ordinary ties; these ties were wafer thin and, with the help of a stud, were held onto our starched collars and folded back in on themselves. An easy target for jokers. A few of the older boys would repeatedly go for some of the younger ones' ties but I, on the other hand, would only do it to my friends. 'Here, Henry, what's that on your neck?' I'd say, then reaching in to point I would grab his tie instead and give it a good yank. Irritating, I'm sure, but I thought it was funny. Moral of the story: always carry a spare.

We had a very regimented schedule. During the week, the day began at 7.30 a.m. when us boys would wash and dress before breakfast. After that, four days a week, we attended Chapel at 8.35 a.m. Around four hundred boys met in the Lower Chapel, where the chaplains conducted a service that was usually about a specific theme and where there was a lot of singing. A great friend of mine, Mazdak Sanii, and I always enjoyed starting the day with a good hymn. It might sound a bit laborious to have to go through so often, but the chaplains always made the time fly, by being witty and light-hearted, so it wasn't all that bad. Looking back on my experiences at Eton, it is difficult not to smile to oneself when remembering the diversity of characters that were on offer in the staffroom. They certainly made life at the school easier.

After classes in the afternoon, boys would go off to do extra work, play sport or attend the societies they were interested in. Supper was at 7.40 p.m. followed by house prayers at about 8.20 p.m. and then lights out. Between house prayers and lights out (9.30 p.m. for F block, which was what the first year was called) you had time to finish off your work for the following day or have a bath or shower or whatever. This was the time when your house-master or dame was likely to drop by your room to have a chat. If you were missing, you needed a good excuse.

Up to GCSE we'd study English and maths, biology, chemistry and physics, also a language or two amongst other things. Latin was also compulsory. The system became a bit looser in sixth form when you could start to branch into more specialist subjects or the subjects you were keen on carrying on. I excelled particularly at theatre studies, art and languages.

After having got off to a slow social start at Trevor-Roberts, I was determined not to go through the same thing at Eton. I wanted to break the mould and start afresh, particularly by losing my Frenchness and becoming more British. It's hard to describe, but there's a distinct difference between boys who've gone through the French educational system – where falling over in the playground can result in a huddle of concerned teachers debating whether to call an ambulance – and boys who've been to sporty British schools where a degree of toughness is automatically acquired. I wanted to be like the latter. Understanding my need to be popular, The Band allowed me to throw a party at the house on Park Street during my first year. House parties were all the rage at that time – we were too young to attempt to get into clubs, and a lot of the under-eighteens' clubs, such as Capital VIP, didn't serve alcohol. Almost all of us were experimenting with alcohol by then – or in some cases had already become thoroughly familiar with it – so teetotal parties were not enticing.

Dad said to me, 'Invite thirty people, and let's have snacks, water, soft drinks and some alcohol, and keep an eye on things, please, Spen.'

I nodded and duly went off and invited sixty people – which I am sure Mum and Dad expected – making sure that all the coolest kids were on my list. On the day of the party, I was walking along the King's Road with a friend, discussing how we were looking forward to the event, when two kids we'd never met before walked past us chatting.

'Are you going to that party on Park Street later?' one asked the other.

My friend looked at me with a slightly surprised expression. 'It looks like there might be more people coming tonight than you realize. I hope things really kick off!'

This sent a chill down my spine. Disobeying The Band at this age meant trouble. I mentioned to my parents that it was just possible a few more people than expected might be coming, so they hired two guys to act as security on the door. It turned out we were right – close to three hundred kids turned up and the guys couldn't cope. Every boy they questioned would claim to be a friend of Emily's, and with every girl it was Will or Tom or whoever. Some kids looked about eighteen. As soon as we opened the door, the house was rammed and the alcohol was consumed by the masses in about six minutes flat. People I had never met and who weren't even at Eton just kept pouring through the door. It was as though each person had invited someone else, and they had invited someone else, and so on. All the kids had mobiles, and we realized they'd all texted their friends about the party, causing the invasion. The only thing I am glad of is that Facebook didn't exist in those days, or perhaps *Project X* would have come out sooner.

As it was, though, the party was insane. Pictures were dislodged from the walls, a girl fainted, drinks were spilt on the carpets . . . it was starting to look as if we were just one step away from people swinging on the chandeliers. It was animalistic, like we were in the middle of the movie *Superbad*. It was time for The Band to intervene and proceedings came to an end. The two of us managed to organize a reasonably orderly departure of the hordes from the house. As we closed the door behind the last reveller, we grinned at each other. That had been a close call. Unsurprisingly, that was my last house party in central London for many years.

As far as my schoolmates were concerned, though, it had been a huge success and got me high fives all round, so it did the job in terms of my social life.

Three boys from Eton rapidly became my closest friends, Michael Simpson, Henry Leech and Tom Brooksbank – and we're all still in touch more than a decade later. Michael was furiously intelligent and worked extremely hard. While he was perhaps my closest friend out of the three, he was sometimes conscious of not getting into trouble, so when it came to misbehaving my partner in crime tended to be Henry. He was an interesting character, being a grade 8 violinist and skateboarder, forever making videos, and was generally up for giving any new thing a go.

Lastly, Tom, who was probably the coolest of the three of us, was very chilled. Tom was the first of us to smoke, and even though he wasn't the best-looking guy in school, he was one of the first to have a girlfriend . . . and then another and another. There's something about his nature that is incredibly endearing and once you spend some time with him you're likely to call him your best friend.

By coincidence, one of my nearest and dearest from my Wellow House days, Michael MacDonald, was also at Eton, but unfortunately we never really picked up our close relationship again, mainly because we weren't in the same house. But also because by then we were heading in different directions: he was interested in academic life, and was good at it too, whilst my head was full of sport and drama. It was lovely to have him so close to me for those five years though, given the times we spent together as children, and he has done really well since leaving the school.

At the end of the first year we went back to St Barths for the holidays, where I was joined by Henry, Tom and Michael. With thoughts of school firmly banished for the time being, we hit the beach, and kept an eye out for any pretty girls who might happen to cross our paths. We did, of course, have the deadly effective Tom with us . . .

At this point in time my luck with girls, or rather my experience with girls, was totally non-existent. I may have applied a bit of topspin to stories I told back at Eton about my expertise with women, but that's what you do in a school full of boys who are out to better each other in the tall tales stakes. These were only white lies, I can assure you.

On one particular day, however, I spotted a beautiful girl out on the sea on a floating wooden raft, owned by Eden Rock. You can swim out to it and dive off it – and as I am writing this, I have just spotted Jessica Alba doing exactly that, looking quite splendid on that same raft with the odd pap snapping away.

Although I was still carrying a few unwanted pounds, I was looking more or less okay and, more importantly, appeared a bit older than I was. As soon as the girl had swum back to the beach I strode up to her and asked her if she would like to join me for a drink or two – one of the many perks of knowing The Band was that I never had to produce any ID. She said yes to my somewhat unprepared approach and smiled, looking even more beautiful close up. Even now, looking back, she is still up there with the best – not one of those childhood romances that you end up regretting. She told me her name was Susannah and that she was on holiday from Puerto Rico with her parents. She also told me that she was sixteen. It was at this point I realized I may have a bit of a mountain to climb, but even in the heat I did my best to keep it cool. Here I was, thirteen years old with lust on the brain, chatting up a girl who was quite obviously out of my league. Having cemented the fact in my own mind that I was also sixteen, and having figured out my new birthday in case she asked me what star sign I was, we moved over to the bar. Conversation flowed freely and before we agreed to head to our separate rooms to change for the evening I had a date – completely forgetting that she'd be joining the rest of the team.

Having told Brooksbank to keep his game to himself, we all headed to the beach for a few drinks. As the night progressed it did become a little awkward. She was in fact a fourth wheel to our boys' night at the beach but the boys were mature for their years and allowed us some space. We got to know each other and felt more relaxed as the sun was beginning to set and the stars were starting to appear across the cloudless skyline. You couldn't imagine a more romantic scene and I knew then and there – and by the fact that she hadn't run away yet – that the signs were looking good for me to make my move, so I did.

As we were speaking I looked deeply into her gorgeous brown eyes, and held her gaze. Suddenly the conversation stopped and I knew it was time. Closing my eyes a little bit, but leaving enough of a gap to see where I was headed, I shared my first real kiss to speak of. It was a special moment – an odd balance between cluelessness and joy – as we lay back in the sand. I didn't want it to end but a couple of the boys were getting a bit restless. After all, I had brought them out to an island and just left them on a beach. We changed location and all proceeded to have fun until the early hours of the following day. I didn't feel the need for more than a kiss at that time in my life. Susannah had made my evening.

After that night, Susannah and I met up again for pizza and enjoyed the next few days. But it was all rather innocent and youthful. Of course, I couldn't stop thinking about that first kiss. From that moment on, I felt more like a man than ever before. In fact, I felt like the king of the world and made sure that my mates listened as I recounted every detail of what had happened on that beach several times over. Obviously my boys played it cool, as if it was something they did themselves every day, which they most certainly didn't – well, maybe Tom occasionally – but I could sense that beneath their poker faces they were happy for me. But, of course, the downside of a holiday romance is that people go home and people move on. However, a milestone had been crossed and a start had been made.

Thanks to my somewhat seamless success with Susannah, I had elevated confidence when it came to talking to girls. I must have been giving off some kind of vibe because a couple of weeks later, something happened that made the first serious kiss pale into insignificance . . .

Since watching *Color of Night*, my sexual appetite had engaged and I had spent years and years dreaming about living that scene out for myself. After kissing Susannah, during which I experienced totally new feelings, I was keener than ever to lose my virginity. Although I was confident I could live up to Brucey's example, I still wasn't quite sure how to find a willing partner.

Most of the people who ran the clubs and bars in St Barths welcomed me into their establishments. I was a familiar face around the island and in many cases they were regulars of ours at Eden Rock. At this time, IDs were never really checked and police in general were next to non-existent. Regardless of the fact I was just thirteen years old, one night I was out on the town with racing driver, British saloon car champion and friend of the family Jason Plato, who was in his mid-thirties at the time. Jason now presents the hit show *Fifth Gear* and is happily married with a lovely wife Sophie and two gorgeous daughters. That evening, he turned to me and said, 'I don't get why you don't take these girls back to the hotel.'

I'm not sure if he had forgotten my age, but he seemed to think it extraordinary that I wasn't chatting up girls left, right and centre and dragging them back to my room. Of course, I had only just experienced my first serious kiss, so the thought of going all the way was slightly daunting, not that I was willing to volunteer that info to worldly-wise Mr Plato.

However, as the evening went on, it became pretty obvious to Jason that my experience with women was limited, so he decided to coach me.

'Look, mate,' he said. 'All you need to do is walk up to a woman you fancy, start talking to her, and when you get into a comfortable conversation just look her in the eye and say, "Let's go back to the hotel," and see how that runs.'

Surely it couldn't be that easy, I thought to myself. If it was, I'd been wasting time. But Jason was adamant, and told me to look around the bar and see if there were any girls there who caught my eye. I spotted a blonde girl with a tanned, slim and sexy body and I could see that she was older than me, but only by a few years. For a moment I fixed my gaze on her, waiting for her to sense me looking at her. Eventually, she looked up and I caught her eye. I flashed her a warm smile and received one in return.

'Go,' Jason said.

Gliding across to the bar, with what I believed to be confidence, I went to join her. We began exchanging chit-chat, while every so often I'd look over to Jason for some sort of security. Once I'd passed the buying the first drink and age test, things became a little easier. As it happened, she was the sister of one of the chefs at the hotel, so the opening conversation was easier than I thought. She also knew the hotel which prompted me to nervously ask the question, 'Shall we go back there for a drink after this?'

After a pause she agreed. She turned to ask the barman something and for the brief moment that her back was turned to me, thumbs up were presented by Jason who was standing by the back wall looking on like a proud father. The plan was in motion. Could this be it?

I explained that it was best she drive as my licence had been suspended, and that I needed to say goodbye to a mate of mine. Jason Plato discreetly handed me my first condom and wished me good luck. I was on my own.

As the door to Spencer's Cabin shut behind us, my heart began beating rapidly, and images of all the porn I'd ever watched seemed to have vanished. Fortunately, and this was as much to do with the girl, there wasn't any awkward lingering for she knew and I knew exactly what the score was . . . Well it wasn't long before I achieved what I'd been longing for since the ripe age of eight. In my eyes, I'd become a man.

In a strange way, though, I was a little bit disappointed with sex. I had heard stories of the endless pleasure sex could provide to both parties and may have built it up a little too much in my mind. This kind of thing happens when you want something badly for so long. Or perhaps the porn stars were just faking it. I did enjoy it, but it wasn't this earth-shattering fanfare and fireworks moment that I had expected. Nevertheless, I was beyond gleeful that I could finally officially say I was no longer a virgin and couldn't wait to tell anyone who'd listen.

A few hours later, we had a brunch to attend as a family at a friend's house. My cousin Luke was there, with whom I still enjoy a good competition even now, and although Luke had long since lost his virginity, he flat out refused to believe me. To be fair, in retrospect, I can see where he would have been coming from. After endless arguing, he still wouldn't accept it and I was forced to drop the subject. *I* knew it was true and wasn't in the mood for any more negative energy. After all, men don't quarrel over such trivial matters.

My sex life really took off that summer, owing to the confidence gained from that first time and to Jason Plato's simple wisdom. I owed this man for what he had taught me. He was my hero. He'd given me some simple but effective advice and, although it was just throwaway to him, to me it felt like he had given me the key to a whole other world. To this day it's still the most direct, effective way of flirting.

What probably helped each time I first made my approach, was that on the outside I would appear to be young, sweet and innocent. So all in all pretty unthreatening. Nine times out of ten it worked, and before the girls could figure out quite what was happening, they'd be back in Spencer's Cabin.

Although it's never easy leaving St Barths behind, I was happy to be back at Eton at the start of September 2001. I'd missed my mates and had plenty to tell them. Mum and Dad were back in London too, staying at Park Street, and on a visit to the house I struck again, though in a different way to the party. It was unintentional, but I came close to getting shot.

The house happened to be opposite the American Embassy and on one particular Saturday night, several hours after I should have been asleep, I was messing around with a laser pen, wondering what it would be good for. Looking out of the window I saw a police officer on guard outside the Embassy – this was soon after the September 11 attacks, so security was particularly high and people were on edge. It seemed as if there were police everywhere, kitted out in bulletproof vests and carrying machine guns.

For some reason, I decided it would be fun to make this one officer believe he was under fire. Hiding out of sight behind my curtain, I shone the laser on his vest and waited. Suddenly he noticed it and began taking ridiculous side steps to get away from it. He would jump to one side, and I would move my pen with him. He jumped back, and the pen followed. Well, that was it. He got on the radio pronto and I could hear him speaking frantically, then he sprinted round the corner and into the Embassy.

I had a little chuckle to myself at his overreaction and was about to get into bed when, literally about a minute after his departure, alarms began to sound. Then I heard sirens approaching and five police cars started piling down Park Street – which is a one-way street – in the wrong direction! Any doubt about where these cars were headed disappeared when they screeched to a halt right outside our door. The policemen leapt out with guns, armed and dangerous. I threw my pen across the room and hopped into bed, thinking that the cover of darkness would be my best option.

Mum came into my room to check if I was okay and I stuck to my sleeping story. But The Band knew something was up and sent for me to join him and the police in the hallway.

'Spencer, boy, do you know something about a laser light?' he asked.

There was a long pause. 'Yes, I do.'

I explained, and the police, who were a tough-looking bunch, relaxed a bit and were very cool actually, although none of them said very much at all. Dad invited me to apologize, which I did with enthusiasm. The police gave nothing away, but jumped back into their cars and roared up the street in the same manner in which they had arrived.

Dad then pointed out to me that so soon after 9/11 the Embassy security and the local armed police were likely to have been given rules of engagement that allowed them, in certain circumstances, to fire back against what they perceived as a threat. He thought what I'd done with the laser had been quite risky. It would have been awkward to have been on the end of a real sniper rifle laser sight. Good thing they held fire.

Above My father, David Matthews, retires from motor racing . . . British Grand Prix meeting, Silverstone 1973.

My beautiful mother Jane. She was nineteen when this was taken, and had just been voted Carnival Queen at Rhodes University, South Africa.

Right Apple of my father's eye!

Below Day One.

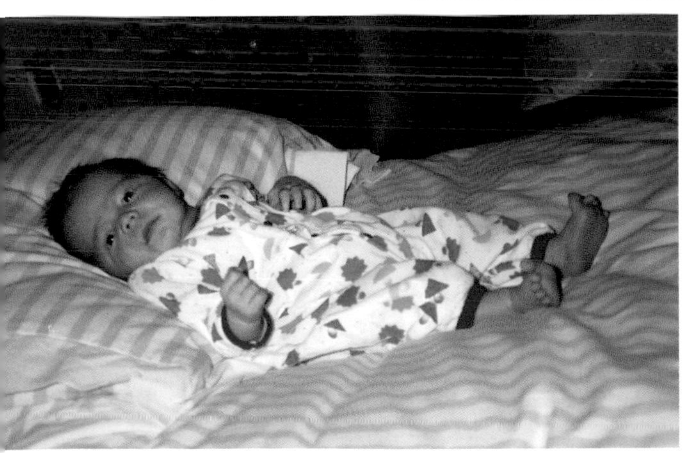

The village garden party at Caunton Manor, summertime, 1989.

With a young Michael MacDonald (right) at Glen Affric, Scotland.

As a young artist, exploring the streets of Paris.

Sailing from Antigua to St Barths in 1995.

Hurricane Luis hits St Barths a few days after we arrive.

Sheltering under the sink with my parents' friends, Leslie and Steve . . .

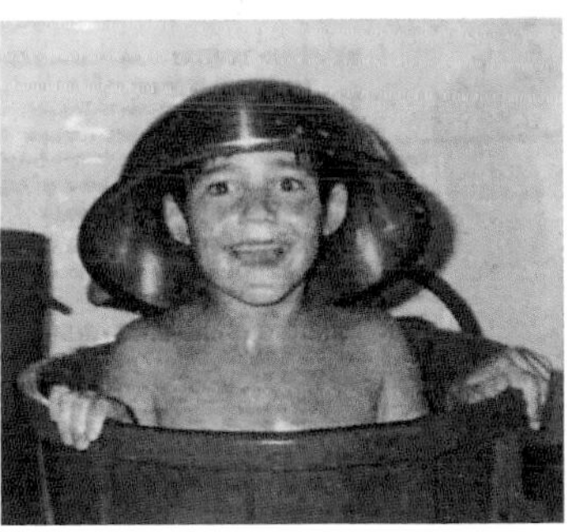

. . . and then finding my own refuge.

Young love: playing on the beach with Meryl and my brother Michael.

Left One of m early painting from St Barth

This photo was taken by a couple of guests at Eden Rock in 1998. When the film was developed, they sent the photo with a note to my parents describing me as an 'irrepressible charmer'. Moments after the photo was taken, I sold the painting to their friend.

Right A family trip to New York.

Even though Michael (below left) and I (below right) were born twelve years apart, everyone has always said how alike we look. This picture of Michael as a choir boy was used for the invites to his twenty-first birthday party in Las Vegas.

My first year at Eton College.

Eton's annual 'Fourth of June' celebration. The oarsmen, dressed up in period naval uniforms, row past the crowds assembled on the riverbank and salute them by standing up and raising their oars. Those who capsize are breathalyzed.

Susannah, a beautiful girl from Puerto Rico, with whom I shared a holiday romance – and my first kiss.

Winning the Head of the River Trophy in the Bumping Fours at Eton. From left to right: Arthur Hughes-Hallett; Henry James; Henry Leech; the headmaster of Eton, Mr Tony Little; me and Michael Simpson.

An AS-level art project.

Aged sixteen – embarrassing hair.

CHAPTER 9

A Shocking Pupil

'In all my years as a teacher, never before have I met a boy quite like Spencer,' Mr Fielker once said to my parents. It's certainly a comment that could be taken in different ways but I like to see it as a compliment because I got on well with the housemaster and his wife Lu – and think highly of them to this day.

You won't find very much – if any – detail on my classes at Eton over the next few chapters. The following quotes from some of my reports might help explain why:

FRENCH REPORT:

> Effort has been practically non-existent and what makes the matter worse is that he openly boasts about how he gets by without doing anything. But I add that although we have done famous battle together, Spencer has been unfailingly cheerful and well-mannered at all times . . . What does one do?

DRAMA REPORT:

Although there are few people with whom, and out of school, I would prefer to sip a cocktail, there is still a tendency to play the fool, which sabotages his chances of a really good mark . . . He is bad at judging when to stop playing around and get down to work.

TUTOR'S REPORT:

Once again Spencer's reports are colourful, if a little bit alarming. They testify to his innate ability, but highlight his inability to work hard. I have never known a boy to inspire masters to write quite such creative and distinctive reports. He seems to encourage his teachers to come up with ever more inventive ways to condemn his inactivity . . . I have enjoyed tutoring Spencer because he is a fun and interesting boy. I do hope that he maintains this charm, but I wish more strongly that he develops a bit more discipline and ambition.

To sum up, I was a shocking pupil. To the frustration of the teachers, I would do no work during term time, which they punished me for, but come the exams I'd study like mad for a week and do well.

There is one particular friend I have to thank for some of this – Mazdak Sanii, a friend I initially made in chapel – who, on leaving school, was recruited straightaway by the Rothschild Bank. He was – and still is – one of the most ridiculously intelligent and interesting people I have ever met. His father is Persian and his mother English. He is strikingly good-looking but, more helpfully, one of his parents was a lecturer at Oxford and the other at Cambridge, and Mazdak inherited intelligence from both of them. He was doing exams at Eton before the expected age and in subjects the school didn't even teach but which he taught himself in his spare time. He would help me a lot through school if I was behind, and in the run-up to exams would make me capable of passing my own papers more effectively than the teachers could. He sailed through his own at the same time, of course.

Although I did okay in exams, my behaviour outside the classroom was frequently reported to our headmaster, Mr Little. I might as well have had my own chair in his office, the amount of time I spent in there. In fact, if I may say so, I ended up seeing him so often that we became sort of friends. With hindsight, I can see he managed me expertly and in a way that ensured I got the most out of my time at Eton, and for that I am profoundly grateful.

There was one occasion when I was particularly impressed by Mr Little's reaction to one of my minor crimes. And even now, looking back on it, I can't believe he responded in the way that he did. Again, it involved a laser pen.

One afternoon, whilst minding my own business in my room – I can't remember if I was doing homework or, more likely, watching *Lost* – a red spot from a laser pen started darting about my computer screen. Now, in fact, I recall that I was watching *Lost*, as the computer was positioned in just about the only place in the room where I'd have time to pull up some work onto the screen if disturbed by a member of authority. Going quickly to the window, I uncovered the source of the rather annoying red speck on my screen – an irritating boy called Bruce in his Eton house across the way. At first I tried to ignore his provocation, and in retrospect should have just closed the curtain, but allowing him to feel that he was succeeding in being irritating was not my style. I remembered that a couple of mates – Henry Leech and Hugh Tyser – had recently purchased a rather handsome catapult. This was not one of those small handheld jobs but an altogether more impressive piece of apparatus. It was a three-man catapult, if you please – one person holds each side, while the third aims and fires. The catapult would make for satisfactory retribution.

Henry and Hugh were game and we set up the equipment at the incredibly small, old-fashioned panel-window and filled a stout balloon with water. Now, at a rough estimate, Bruce's room was about fifty or so yards away, over two gardens, two pavements and a road – so an impossible distance. This meant that we had to aim perfectly and ensure that we worked the catapult expertly to have any chance of even exiting our window safely let alone hitting the house, never mind getting close to Bruce. So with Henry and Hugh holding each side of the catapult, I placed the fat water bomb in the cradle and pulled it back as far as I could – and some. I was pulling so hard that my core started to shake. The boys were beginning to have trouble keeping the catapult stable.

'For fuck's sake, Spenny!' snapped Henry.

The shot had to be perfect, I was in the zone. Bruce could see what we were doing but was unfazed due to the ridiculous distance. With the laser light on my chest, I decided it was time to take the shot. I let go and it felt like the whole world went quiet. The bomb cleared our window perfectly and tore through the air gracefully, arcing over the impossible distance. It reached the house and hit Bruce's window, shattering the glass and drenching Bruce, his laptop and his laser pen with water. We couldn't believe it. Victory had never been so sweet.

But our jubilation was diminished when we saw Bruce's housemaster was heading over. He stormed across the gardens and the road, and demanded of our housemaster that he find the culprits. So good Mr Fielker did the rounds, eventually stopping at my door to ask if I knew anything about the water bomb.

My first thought was to plead ignorance in the hope we could bluff our way out of it, as I didn't fancy getting hauled up again before the headmaster. But if there was one thing I knew about our housemaster, it was that he wouldn't rest until the culprits were found. Also, I could hear The Band's voice ringing in my head telling me that, as a rule, less trouble would be encountered if I told the truth.

Dad once told me a story about Mike during his school days at Uppingham, when he and a group of other senior boys picked up the matron's car, and carried it from the front of the house, where it was parked, around to the back, where they placed it neatly in the middle of the vegetable patch. The next day the house was lined up while the housemaster shouted, 'Of course, this won't be the work of any of you, will it?' before pausing for effect.

Quietly and firmly, and with a little smile, Mike said, 'Actually, it was me, sir.'

The rest of the boys owned up too, and as a result their punishment was less severe, and it was felt they had gained the moral high ground – and so had won!

I had always been proud of that story – the bit about how they managed to move the car, that is. But Dad quoted it as an example of integrity, and not being afraid to tell the truth, and I couldn't help but think of this at that moment with Mr Fielker.

'I did it, sir.' The words tumbled out and Mr Fielker looked at me uncertainly.

'But how did you do it? The distance, that is?'

I replied that I was alone in my actions but on overhearing this Henry and Hugh joined my side. I have to say that Mr Fielker was intrigued by the accuracy of this three-man catapult, being a physics beak.

We were sent off to see Mr Little. In his office I began to feel nervous. It was sinking in that we had attacked a fellow student, had damaged school property and possibly could have really hurt Bruce with the broken glass. I had a funny feeling we were going home for a few days.

Mr Little studied us, glancing from Henry to Hugh and

back to me again. 'Who actually fired the thing?' he enquired.

'I did, sir.'

Mr Little dismissed the other two boys and invited me to sit down. I'd lost my wingmen.

'So, you're telling me that from your room, you shot a balloon at Bruce's window.'

'I am, sir.'

'You sent a water-filled balloon at least fifty yards from your room?'

'Yes, sir.'

'And you hit this chap's window.'

'Yes, sir.'

'Why did you do it?'

I explained how the laser pen was disrupting my workflow – Mr Little knew I wasn't working – and how irritated I felt by Bruce and his determined effort to provoke me.

Mr Little sat back in his chair. 'Well,' he said slowly. 'Good shot.'

What a fine response from the headmaster of Eton.

Later, I joined Eton's shooting eight and was in the first pair for three years. I very much enjoyed shooting, especially at Bisley and other such magnificent grounds, and the guys on the team were good company too.

As well as shooting, I played tennis. Oliver Proudlock, despite being in the year above, ended up opposite me one lovely afternoon and we started playing together. Ollie would become one of my best friends and a fellow *Made in Chelsea* alumnus. Proudlock, as he is now known, was great at sport and highly popular at Eton. He was always busy taking trips to Cornwall or Portugal or whatever holiday spot was cool at the time. He's what you might have called a trendsetter – what happened?

So on this particular day during our match, Proudlock asked me, over the net, 'Doesn't your dad have that hotel in St Barths?'

'Yeah. You should come out at some point,' I said casually.

In a matter of days, Proudlock had called to tell me he'd booked his flight and would be joining me for the summer. If he wasn't such a popular, nice guy I would have said he was taking advantage. As it happens, I was delighted to have him. When he arrived, the holiday was destined for great times and I knew that we would develop a lasting friendship.

That same summer I was at La Luna one night (now called The Yacht Club) in Gustavia, the capital of St Barths and where most of the fun is to be had on the island. I started chatting to a rather attractive French girl named Simone. She asked where I was from and then what I did in London. At this time in my life I was still pretending to be older, which meant I needed a career. On that particular night, I decided I was a racing driver. This was a pretty cool job and, coming from a racing family, I knew some of the right things to say. So there I was, telling her all about what it was like to race for Manor Motorsport (now managing the Marussia F1 team). When it was time to make the necessary move to take Simone home, we walked out – and she threw her car keys at me.

'Here, racing driver, you drive! You'll do a better job than me, even after a few drinks!'

Fuck! I'd never driven a full-sized car in my life, but never one to turn down a challenge, I decided I could mentally talk myself through it. Driving was surely in my blood. Walking round to the driver's side of the white Suzuki, I saw it was an automatic. First hurdle overcome. I was so worried the car would jump as I turned it on that I simultaneously put the key in the ignition and slammed my foot on the brake so hard it was nearly through the floor. As I twisted the key, the hum of the engine began. *Okay*, I thought, *we're getting somewhere here. Now put the car into drive as you've seen people do.*

Slowly, I pulled forward and gently took the first bend, and then the second. It was just like driving a go-kart but I didn't want to treat the streets of St Barths like a track, especially when driving illegally. Simone wasn't particularly impressed with my driving and urged me to show off my skills as a professional. My arm had been twisted.

All the places on St Barths are really close together – generally you are hard-pushed to find anywhere that you can't drive to in ten minutes – so I thought *drive quicker, get home sooner, no problem.*

Everything I had heard James discuss with The Band during race days was flooding into my slightly drunken mind – pointing into corners early, accelerating early out of them, looking for the racing line to be fast – I tried them all, and soon thought that driving a full-sized car was no problem at all.

Simone's house, however, was about the only place on the island that was not nearby. In fact, I didn't even know where it was. Leading to her house was a long straight road, and with no other cars in sight, I was building up some speed. I accelerated hard to get over a hill, but as it dipped I kept my foot down, not realizing how fast we were going. Suddenly, a sharp right appeared from nowhere and I tried to turn into it but we were going way too fast and skidded across the road sideways into a barrier. As we went up on two wheels, Simone flew across the car, clashing heads with me and smashing us into the side window. It shattered, covering us with glass, before the car banged and scraped its way downwards again. We sat in shock for a minute, then climbed out to see that on the other side of the barrier was the edge of a high cliff. Without the barrier, it could have been curtains for us.

We tried to move the car, but it wasn't functioning.

'You should go home,' she said quickly. 'I think it is best for both of us if I say I was driving.'

Relief washed over me in an awesome wave (kind of like when Patrick Bateman gets his decent table at Espace). 'Really? I'm happy enough to face the music,' I said solemnly, but also keen, if that was to be the plan, to get moving before her parents came out to investigate the noise. I hitched a ride home, as everyone does in St Barths.

So that was my night as a racing driver cut short. I have

seen Simone since and we have had a few dates. We still laugh about our scare and she is a great girl – and I'm a grateful boy.

Unfortunately this wasn't the only time I found myself bloodied and sore on the roadside that summer. The second incident involved Hercule, the iguana and icon of the hotel, who seemed to go mad overnight. There was a lunar eclipse, and I don't know if that was a contributory factor, but it seemed as if the next day he turned angry and aggressive. No longer happy to come and be fed, or pose for photos, instead he would chase guests, appearing from within the bushes, and running at them baring his big talons, or lashing out with his tail. I know first-hand how much that can hurt after he caught me as I roller-bladed past him, leaving my legs with cuts and grazes that took weeks to heal.

There was no coaxing out the old Hercule that summer, and as he was becoming a bit of a bore, it was decided that it was time for him to retire. Dad bundled him into his pick-up truck and released him on the other side of the island – the windward side where fewer people live. Perhaps the fame had got to him.

Starting back on another term at Eton, the adventures continued when Henry, Tom, Michael and I decided to give Bekynton, the cafeteria, a bit of a makeover. What made it a little different from the rest of the buildings on campus was that it had a glass roof. So, if you were to look up from the array of breakfast cereals on offer, you would be able to see up into the morning sky. This, in our view, was not interesting enough.

Late one night, the four of us climbed quietly onto the roof of the building armed with bagfuls of pornos and glue. We started pulling out the pages of the magazines and plastered the X-rated images facedown all over the glass roof. It was great fun and we covered the whole lot quickly.

Sadly, we were not there to see it for ourselves, but we heard that the explicit pictures were spotted by the first boy to breakfast, and then there was total chaos as the rest of the boys clambered onto tables to get a closer look.

Needless to say, an enquiry was launched but luckily suspicion never came our way, as the Eton authorities assumed that the guilty parties were regular users of the cafeteria. So we were free and clear.

When we weren't playing pranks, we would try to drift off campus and head into Windsor or London for a night out. But attempts to do this constituted quite serious rule-breaking and so we needed to plan carefully.

To ensure these rules were adhered to, the school sometimes had teachers or, more usually, members of Pop installed on the bridge that led across to Windsor. Pop is the name given to the Eton Society which comprises the highest kind of prefect. It is an honour to be chosen to join Pop, and it used to be the case that students would determine Poppers based on a person's popularity and, often, their sporting prowess. As you can imagine, many of the Poppers, from across the different year groups, didn't exactly meet the standards of what a school prefect should be in the eyes of authority. In my day, old Pop was the right Pop. These students were respected throughout the school and listened to by those in lower years. But now Pop is determined almost entirely by the college, with academic achievement – combined perhaps with one's ability to play an instrument – being considered. I'm not saying that people in Pop currently do not deserve to be in Pop, but I will say that there was a fairly drastic change to the system during our time at Eton, and that it may be more difficult now for Poppers to demand respect from other students than it was then.

So anyway, Poppers were placed on the bridge at certain hours to keep an eye out for younger students heading into Windsor. Of course they'd let some people in their own year slide – that was just part of the way things worked – but we had to be smart. To avoid detection we would dress to go out, then throw a hoodie on top. When we approached the bridge, we'd pull the hoods over our heads, light a cigarette each and walk with an ASBO swagger to give the impression that we were anything other than Eton students. More often than not it would work and we'd end up spending an evening at the local nightclub, Liquid, or the Crown and Cushion pub on the high street.

Of course, there were times when we were caught. Once it happened to me after what must have been a particularly good evening. I don't really remember now where I had been or how I actually ended up lying in the street asleep. According to eyewitnesses, I was rather the worse for wear and had fallen over while skipping back to the house. Finding the pavement surprisingly comfortable, I dropped off. The next thing I remember is being roughly shaken awake by a large and unsympathetic teacher, Mr Rose. Next stop – Mr Little.

Other nights, Michael and I would venture into London and hit the clubs. Being underage, we thought some facial hair might help to get past the bouncers. But finding it hard to grow proper facial hair, the two of us came up with the idea of cultivating these footballer-esque goatees, Pirez strips, as we called them. Unfortunately, even these strips were tough to grow at such a young age, and more often than not, they'd fail to materialize. Michael is still trying to grow one today, ten years later! Back then, our attempts were so pathetic that we may or may not have enhanced them with a swipe or two of mascara which, looking back, would have been embarrassing had we done it – which we didn't. That said, our Pirez strips must have worked quite well because we seemed to have no problem getting into high-end London clubs at the time, like Tantra. Perhaps they felt sorry for us. After all, we did make an effort.

But while it was all well and good gaining entrance to clubs full of glamorous people, at this age we had the further disadvantage of having very little money to play with. When I was fifteen, my parents began to give me £150 a month, from which I had to buy toiletries, food and so on. And when it ran out, it really ran out! Michael was in the same boat. So, for example, on a typical 'luxury' night out, we'd spend £20 on a taxi, £20 to get into the club and £15 to buy a drink. We wouldn't be left with enough money to buy drinks for girls as well, so within ten minutes of stepping through the door the cash had dried up and after a couple of nights out like that a month we'd be pretty much penniless until our next payday.

CHAPTER 10

The Escapist

Although I enjoyed meeting girls in London nightclubs and the bars of Windsor, the encounters were always casual – and I found myself getting rather tired of it all. For the first time I wanted someone to love. It's probably not what you'd expect from me, but even a fifteen-year-old with an overdeveloped sexual appetite wants a proper girlfriend.

Step forward Ascot Girl. I was at a rugby game when, having probably just run in the try of the season (wishful thinking), I came across my angel for the next few years. Not only was she beautiful, with blonde hair and bright blue eyes, she was confident and witty, and one of the most popular girls at nearby St George's, a girls' boarding school in Ascot. She was the entire package and I knew it, as did everyone at Eton, so imagine how pleased I was when things began to move in the right direction.

We started dating and had a really great time; it was a wonderful first relationship. She seemed one of a kind and we had a lot of fun together. I took her to restaurants – if funds allowed – or we'd go for drinks or walks around our respective campuses. We also used to hang out with her girlfriends, one of whom happened to be going out with this guy who could only be described as having an odd dress sense, Mr Jamie Laing. Yes, ma boi! He wasn't quite into his sleeveless Yves St Laurent leopard prints yet – or perhaps he just couldn't pull them off at this point. He was the year below at Radley and was an excellent rugby player; he still holds many records within the Radley sporting community, and may have even been good enough to play fullback for the England under-16s – or so he says. Although years later Jamie would end up becoming one of my nearest and dearest, we didn't see each other so much at that point because we'd both be off spending time alone with our girlfriends or respective schoolmates.

Every so often, Ascot Girl would come and visit my room at Eton, which was a risky exercise as sneaking girls onto campus was most definitely frowned upon at school. Now, there was a rumour kicking around while I was there, or it might just be an urban legend, but apparently at Eton if you are caught having sex with a girl in your room you are expelled, but if you're caught with a boy, you just get suspended. But don't hold me to that. It may be just the local leg-pull. In my time no one was expelled for any kind of sex, to my knowledge. Perhaps Etonians are naturally too devious to get caught.

Anyway, trying to sneak Ascot Girl into the house was always something of a production. She'd have to slip away from St George's and, to fool anyone she might encounter along the way, would creep to our house dressed in a hoodie so she looked a little more boyish. After lights out, the main door locked automatically at a set time and couldn't be opened again until the following morning, unless disarmed by activating, say, the fire alarm. So to ensure the door was still in action, we'd quietly stick really thick industrial tape across the locking mechanism. It would still make the usual clicking noise when the door closed so that the dame was none the wiser, but it wouldn't lock properly, thus giving us the opportunity to come and go as we pleased, or to let people in or out.

Even after I'd snuck Ascot Girl into my room there was still a real danger of being caught. There were no locks on the doors of our rooms, which meant someone could walk in while you were otherwise engaged – and people did walk in on us, regularly, though luckily not the housemaster or dame. If they had, my days at Eton may well have been numbered. And that would have been a shame as I would never have achieved the crowning pinnacle of my sporting career . . .

Outside of the classroom I enjoyed rowing and became a senior member of the house Bumping Fours team, having experienced it the year before as a junior. This event is a traditional annual boat race that has taken place between Eton houses since 1902. Each of the twenty-five houses has a boat, with four rowers and a cox, two senior boys and two junior boys in each boat, typically the stockier, stronger boys as technique seldom comes into this race, which is a competition of brawn. The equipment is not what you'd find at Dorney Lake, Eton's main rowing facility, but rather large heavy wooden boats that are difficult to get going, even in the best of circumstances. Around the time of the Bumping Fours, most boys at the school flock to an otherwise unused part of the river, each wearing their respective house colours, thus bringing their support to the banks. The boats are lined up on the river, an equal distance apart, with each starting in the position their house finished in the year before. As the rowers assemble, an air of tension and excitement descends.

Each boat is held in place by a piece of rope, and when a horn is blown, the cox releases it and the race begins. The atmosphere at this point becomes electric. The aim is to catch the boat of the house in front of you, and to physically bump them. If you manage to do this, you move up a place and your race is finished for the session. The other boats continue until they also hit someone else, or finish the course, which can be up to three kilometres long, depending on where you start. It is also possible to double-bump, whereby if the boat that you bump then bumps the boat ahead, you'll jump two spots, etc.

Tactics, such as whether to row at 100 per cent from the off, or to hold back and then make a sudden surge forward when you think the boat in front could be waning, can make all the difference, as once you've burnt out in a rowing boat there's little to no chance of getting back in the race, particularly in these heavy four-man teams. This event is as much a battle of strength of mind as it is of physical strength. Each individual's effort makes a significant difference to the outcome.

The race runs over three evenings, so if you have a good team you can climb several places on the leaderboard, but a bad team can set the house back years. That year our team comprised Michael and me from the senior years, and Arthur Hughes-Hallett and Henry James from the year below. Henry was coxing.

Having started in third place, by the final night we were sitting in pole position, but unlike in Formula One or any other kind of racing, pole position is actually a disadvantage as, for the first time, we would have to finish the entire course. The boat behind us was PSTW, a house at Eton renowned for its rowing. The four sitting in the boat behind us were better rowers than us and had come up from eighth place to second. Things weren't looking great. We had no choice but to give it everything we had from the start and hope for the best. Our boat was certainly the heavier, but arguably the stronger too.

The horn went and we fired out of the traps like greyhounds. Unfortunately, the PSTW team had a similar strategy in mind and came within feet of the stern of the boat almost immediately, but hope was not lost and we pulled as hard as four could pull. Gradually the three-foot lead turned to six feet, then a boat length and then two, until we realized that they were spent. I don't recall whether or not they got bumped due to exhaustion but we crossed the line with a comfortable lead – we had nothing left in the tank, nothing left to give. It was undoubtedly my proudest achievement while at Eton. Competition between houses is rife at public school and this event in particular has an enormous turnout.

I'll never forget the moment when the headmaster presented us with the Head of the River trophy. It was such an honour, an experience that very few people get to take away with them from Eton, and sharing it with Michael, Henry and Arthur made it all the more special.

After some of the usual last-minute cramming, I passed my GCSEs in the summer of 2004. Back at Eton in September, and now in the sixth form, I selected drama, art and French as A-level subjects. I adored drama and studied for four years under the tutelage of Mr Simon Dormandy, a brilliant actor in his own right. I wouldn't say that he exactly inspired me to become an actor – my love of acting was ingrained much earlier on – but he encouraged his students to take the subject seriously, and I enjoyed his classes even though I knew that he was occasionally disappointed by my written work.

On a weekly basis, our drama group would go to see plays and performances around the country, which were wonderful occasions, and characterize the generosity of Eton. We also assembled our own productions, including one called *The Fame Game*, which a small team and I wrote and produced for our AS-level practical exam. It was inspired by George Orwell's *1984*, amongst other sources, in that we experimented with how difficult it was to escape the eye of society nowadays. Writing and then inhabiting such complex roles helped to broaden our horizons – and this project was perhaps my most enriching artistic experience at the school. Given that the team was small we were playing several characters each, constantly dipping from one into another. One of my characters was a girl who had been sexually abused and abandoned by those closest to her. By the time the day came to present to the external examiner, the production was still bitty in places, which is often the case with projects such as these where you are constantly making changes. But the originality of the piece and the peculiarity of its nature must have made for quite an entertaining show as we received a high A.

My love for acting developed during this period, and I knew that performance was something I wanted to pursue, whether appearing in front of the camera, or working on productions behind the scenes.

Perhaps one of the less relevant things to do with my time in sixth form was Eton's insistence that every boy spend part of his spare time in the Army Corp (formally known as the Combined Cadet Force), or doing social services. I opted for the Corp, and while parts of the training were interesting, my sense of humour began to fail after several afternoons spent assembling rifles, standing in formation and generally being regimented. I started to envy those friends with certain food allergies, as nuts were so easily obtainable.

It's not that I enjoyed being disruptive, it's just that I had trouble taking the rigmarole seriously. There were times when I found it difficult not to trip up the person marching in front, hoping for some kind of domino effect. The sergeants would regularly bollock me, but the whole thing felt so pointless that it was like water off a duck's back.

One long weekend we were sent off to northern England for training. It was freezing and few people were having a good time. During one of the exercises in the woods, a sergeant handed out camo paint in green, brown and black and instructed us to put a couple of lines under our eyes – for what I could only imagine was a pointless purpose. This was too good an opportunity to miss. If I was going to 'camouflage' myself – from whom or what I'm not quite sure – I was going to do it properly. The black paint was applied to my entire face, neck, hands and forearms. And once my beret was firmly in place I was indeed unrecognizable. I then patiently waited for the paint to dry completely before applying two green lines underneath my eyes as requested initially. Spencer Matthews had left the building.

The whistle blew and we all had to get into a single line to have our camo paint checked. The sergeant, who wasn't really familiar with any of our names or faces, walked past, studied me, nodded, and walked on.

Then he called the register – what we called absence.

When he got to 'Matthews!' I stayed silent.

'Matthews!!' the sergeant bellowed louder.

I suddenly realized that this joke was going to backfire but it was far beyond the point of no return. I'll keep quiet, I thought to myself. However, all the boys knew where I was, and smiles and light laughter ensued, which sent the sergeant over the edge. 'Where is Matthews?!' he screeched, walking up and down the line, staring everyone straight in the eyes, including me. He was only about six feet away. Of all the people in the world I'd chosen to play a joke on I'd picked the squarest, most within the lines and least likely to be amused individual possible.

Suddenly I couldn't hold it in any longer and burst out laughing. He turned to me and, probably feeling somewhat humiliated, did the unthinkable and kicked me out of Corp. He informed me that he never wanted me in or around any sort of CCF activity ever again – which was mission accomplished.

There was an organized CCF exhibit in front of family and friends due to be held on the main lawn in front of college three days later. We'd been prepping for this event for some time but, as you can probably imagine, I hadn't been given any sort of major role, so it's not as if I'd be missed. In fact, whether I was there or not wouldn't make the slightest bit of difference to the presentation – which is something else I'd found irritating about the CCF in the run up to the event. But now I was free. I headed off to call my parents, wanting to save them a wasted trip. However, The Band decided to attend anyway because he likes that kind of thing, and so he, Mum and I watched as a family from the nearby bar.

I fully expected Eton to insist I start doing social services instead, but for whatever reason my eviction from the

Corp went unnoticed. For the rest of sixth form, while my friends were off polishing their boots, I had the luxury of endless free time.

CHAPTER 11

The African Scam

My relationship with Ascot Girl ended at the beginning of the first year of sixth form. We had enjoyed a great eighteen months together, although like any young couple we had our arguments and a few temporary break-ups. But overall we got on really well and it was a good first try. I will never forget her and the wonderful times we spent together.

There probably wasn't a specific reason why we split; my problem is that once something falls into a routine – whether it's a relationship, lessons or, now, work – I tend to become bored. It's my cross to bear! It's certainly no reflection on Ascot Girl.

Michael and I decided it was time to revisit the club scene at this point. We headed into town, hoping that we'd have more luck than during those days of the dodgy facial hair (a phase very much forgotten by then). Our success rate still wasn't great. Better than most people our age but there was room for improvement, certainly. We'd rock up to places such as Tantra, looking like schoolboys but pretending to be investment bankers, and girls could tell the difference, partially due to our meagre, almost non-existent allowances. Michael's choice of garments didn't help matters either. He had a penchant for a white jacket that he insisted made him look suave, often mixed with a pink shirt, which made him look, say, a bit *Miami Vice* for London – or Henley at the wrong time of year. Not that I know a thing about fashion.

I had more success with girls during the summer holidays that year. First of all, my brother James asked me to go away with him and a few mates, one of whom included Mike's good friend and now a treasure to the family, Aussie Bob. It looked set to be a great trip: the plan was to ride Harley Davidsons in South Africa for two weeks, staying at roadside motels, travelling and exploring by day, drinking and partying by night. As my birthday's not until August, I hadn't yet turned seventeen, didn't have a motorcycling licence and therefore wasn't eligible for my own bike – but I could sit on the back of any of the other guys'. These bikes were beautiful – big and heavy with soft tails, smooth to ride, super-fast and comfortable too. Ideal for the sort of distances we'd be covering. Taking in Africa was a wonderful experience. The landscapes were vast and beautiful, and the conditions absolutely perfect. The accommodation along the way was questionable but I felt like one of the boys on this trip, and was sporting a white leather jacket most of the time – thinking I was a biker.

We partied hard, without restraint, to the point where I

was delighted not to be able to drive. On one particular occasion, staying awake on the back of the bike was too much to ask, so with the help of a few belts and my helmet securely fastened, I fixed my upper body to my brother's back for the entirety of my morning nap. He was no doubt thrilled to bear the extra weight. I resurfaced to find that we were casually cruising down a motorway with the most show-stopping view of land, mountain and sea. What a lovely place to wake up.

To make the journey more interesting, Aussie Bob declared that being in his early thirties, the prime of his life, and having just got over a serious relationship, he was in a strong position to get laid and offered up a wager that he could sleep with the most women on the trip. Most men back themselves, and the rest of us took up the challenge. This had suddenly become a very laddish holiday, but in retrospect all of us were single, close friends, and looking to enjoy ourselves.

By the time we reached our final destination of Johannesburg, Aussie Bob and I were sharing the lead. As this was the end of our tour, we had treated ourselves to one of the city's finest hotels – thanks, James. That evening we walked into the hotel bar, which was full of stunning women – it's rare to find such an accumulation of gorgeous girls in one room at any one time. This was surely going to be the place where the winner of our competition would be decided. No sooner had we bought drinks than one of the women strode up and stroked my face. She made it clear that she was really into me. It seemed reasonable as I was wearing my favourite shirt. I could feel the win was attainable. I was making more progress than Bob. No sooner had I met this woman than she was asking me whether or not I had a room in the hotel. We finished our drinks and disappeared off. I didn't even have to go into detail about my training to be an astronaut, or anything else for that matter.

On the way out, I caught Bob's eye and he laughed. Later I would learn why.

The girl took me by the hand and pulled me upstairs to my room, where she stripped off before undressing me. So far so good. We had sensational sex. Part of me wanted to stay in the room and share a drink, and part of me wanted to get back to the bar to see how Bob was getting on. I tested the water with, 'Would you like to head back down and get another drink?' – killing two birds with one stone. To which she replied in a very relaxed manner, 'Sure. After you give me my hundred rand.'

My heart sank. Not only had I never slept with a prostitute, which I never thought I would, but I'd unintentionally played outside the rules as of course professional girls didn't count. I'd wasted a huge amount of time on the final night when it mattered most. And worst still, I'd left Bob all alone to play the field without competition. However, I had to tend to the matter in hand and figure out how to handle the fact that I'd been scammed. Reflecting on this now, of course she was a professional, but how was I to know? No wonder Bob was laughing.

I refused to pay her, which she didn't like at all. She

picked up the phone to hotel security to say she was experiencing some difficulty with one of their guests. Part of me thought that the 'she never told me she was a prostitute' excuse would get me off the hook with the four large men who appeared in the room within moments. This, unfortunately, was not to be the case. One of the larger men grabbed me by the throat and wrestled me into the bathroom where he proceeded to explain that the only practical way out of this was to pay the girl. I was uncomfortable with this as I dislike not having options, but I understood it was necessary to end this nightmare. I asked the man to calm down and explained that I would pay her, and then proceeded to add that within the confines of my beautiful room I didn't actually have the money. Everyone began taking offence at this. The nightmare was back on. Then, almost by divine intervention, just as the large man was being joined by his three friends in the bathroom, there was a knock on the door. Aussie Bob had arrived.

Bob, worldly-wise guy that he is, had realized that she was a professional from the word go, and predicting a little trouble, had left the competition playground to come and check that everything was okay. It most certainly was not and I will always be grateful to Bob for stepping in that night – a real friend. Bob paid the woman and the competition ended up a tie. We shook hands and agreed that we had very much enjoyed our time in South Africa together.

*

After the South Africa trip, it was back to St Barths for the rest of the summer – where another encounter with a girl was to have further unexpected consequences.

I do not condone any of the things that follow in this particular chapter, but want to be honest about my life so far – and, like most kids, I have done some pretty stupid things while experimenting.

The Band had decreed that I work during the summer break, so I joined the team of very hard-working Portuguese men who were rebuilding Eden Rock's main house – pretty much – from scratch. I found the construction site surprisingly interesting, particularly the building structures in the new foundation of the house. No hurricane would knock this over.

I was sharing lodgings with a guy called Leo, a friend of mine who I had met on the island. We became close and I got him a job as the Eden Rock's chauffeur. He fitted the part perfectly, spoke two languages with confidence and was a very good-looking and apparently well-rounded character. Every day after work, Leo and I would head down to the beach with a cold beer or two and smoke the weed which he always had on him. Nothing strong – island stuff. That was the extent of my drug experience at that point in time. The two of us headed into town one night, met a couple of girls and brought them back to our room. As we lay about, one of the girls piped up and asked if there was any way she could get some 'stuff'. At first I thought she meant weed, but then it became apparent that she was after something stronger.

I was naive about the drug scene back then, in that I knew what cocaine was but had never seen or used it. 'Yes, just a second,' said Leo, and the next thing I knew he had whipped out this white powder and started cutting it into lines. I immediately thought of *Requiem for a Dream* and how depressing and dark the drug scenes were in that film. I had never understood the appeal of hard drugs.

I looked up to Leo at the time, and although in no way am I saying he misled me – I make my own decisions – somehow seeing him do it made it seem okay. I knew taking cocaine wasn't right or something I needed to do, and like most parents, mine had warned me away from drugs. But sometimes people want to experience things for themselves even if they know it won't be a regular occurrence. I'm not usually one to succumb to peer pressure but when one of the girls came up for breath and asked if I was going to join them and have a line, everything started to happen really quickly. Leo and both girls seemed unaltered and the room was energetic and fun, and before I knew it I'd done my first line.

Drugs in this part of the world are renowned for being clean and pure, so what we were taking was strong. But much like the feeling when I lost my virginity, I was expecting so much more – some sort of mind-altering mood swing. The only difference I noticed was that I was *engaged* in the conversation, which, I might add, when you're trying to get with a girl can only be a good thing. I found myself being interested in absolutely everything she had to say, from work to horse-riding to whatever. I needed to know every detail and she seemed similarly fascinated by me. The sex was heightened and I was enjoying myself – and not paying any attention to the dangers that could ensue from enjoying myself a little too much.

This experience repeated itself more regularly than I anticipated over the summer. I do not condone drugs and am uncomfortable about appearing to glamorize them, but as I've decided to write this book, I need to tackle the subject with total honesty.

As a result of the partying and a total loss of appetite, I shed all my puppy fat and looked rather lean by the end of the summer. Having such a low body fat percentage was something I didn't mind at all. Also, given that I was working on a construction site, I'd become extremely tanned. I didn't get any calls from Calvin Klein though.

In fact, this newfound body may well have been one of the reasons my seventeenth birthday went so well.

Directly opposite Eden Rock is Nikki Beach, a crisp, white haven for the world's jet-setters, stars and lovers of life, with vast sunbeds, chic drapery and the beach club's trademark teepees throughout. Given how close it was to home, I was a regular and it's where I celebrated my seventeenth birthday with family and friends.

While sipping a cocktail and enjoying delicious sushi rolls, I looked around and saw that a couple of famous people were present: Enrique Iglesias and Tara Reid, the gorgeous star of *American Pie*, a favourite film of mine whilst at school. Personally, I thought she looked great in the *Big Lebowski*. I chatted with them and both seemed nice, although I felt I had more in common with Tara.

In the back of my mind I thought I would ask her out later. I no longer really feared rejection, having adopted a nothing ventured, nothing gained mentality. It's win-win to be confident; you've got to think that if the lady in question says no then you had no chance in the first place. Try not to waste your time wondering. But first I had to tackle the obvious obstacles. My age would be a problem so I swiftly made my way into the kitchen and asked Nico the chef to please change the big 17 on the extravagant coconut cake to 23. This came as a slight surprise to the family but if they guessed what was going down, they made no mention of it and the laughter continued.

Around five o'clock in the evening, as the heat was diminishing, I went back over to speak to Tara. She was up for chatting – I think the British accent comes in handy when you're trying to charm someone from overseas, and Eton does no harm either. Tara and I were cracking on with a bottle of champagne when she began to talk about Eden Rock, as it was sitting beautifully right in front of us. I'm not one to use The Band's pride and joy to my benefit but when someone tees you up like that it's difficult to ignore. I may have owned the Eden Rock just for a few days.

I wanted to get to know her better and, of course, fancied her, so suggested that she come back to the hotel for a drink at one of the bars. Over we went and sat down drinking Dom Pérignon while chatting about all sorts of things. After a while The Band, Mum and James, who were obviously guests in my hotel, came and joined us for a few drinks. Then I suggested dinner in town. It turns out she was staying with some American friends on their boat so after dinner we ended up back there and let's just say we had a lovely time. We saw each other often during that summer and since then have spent some time in St Tropez together. Tara is a star and full of life and energy and humour.

CHAPTER 12

The Bearded Man

Although my appearance had changed drastically over the course of the summer vacation, I didn't expect as monumental a reaction as the one received upon returning to Eton in September. Everyone kept commenting on how well I looked. It was welcome but the fact of the matter was that I was actually feeling quite ill. Perhaps I'd indulged too hedonistically over the summer but the sudden shock of being back at school didn't seem normal. I felt as though I had the flu or some sort of bug. It was very uncomfortable. The dame also noticed that things weren't quite right. This was certainly no false alarm and off to the sanatorium I went. The GPs allocated to the college are wonderful men, on the case from day to day, and always alert. At first they just suggested rest as they weren't sure what was wrong with me. I had no infection or disease, I was simply unwell. One doctor, who would come up and see me frequently, did ask me whether or not the weight loss was linked with substances of any kind and told me that the information would be strictly confidential. I told him the truth about my summer and he advised taking on board lots of fluids and just sitting it out and eating well.

In a weird way, that episode helped me gain a far greater understanding of drugs and how not to do them. It made me understand the importance of not becoming dependent on anything. Fortunately, as fate would have it, I've always been able to pick stuff up and put it down. I do not have an addictive personality and have always been able to control my actions.

Having said that, my experimentation with substances didn't end with that summer. There was another far darker episode just a couple of months later that really made me question my sanity, and I'm glad to say that this was – and always will be – a one-off.

It was described to me as 'the party of the year', so how could I resist when Oliver Proudlock invited me over to his mother's country pad and told me that we were both going to a large private rave – I didn't realize the two went hand in hand.

We arrived in the middle of a field, complete with bales of hay scattered about the place and bathtubs filled with cans of beer and other alcohol. The night was very much in full swing when we arrived. Everyone was off their face. The music was heavily pumping and it was bordering on pitch black. Proudlock and I got stuck in. Things were about to take a turn for the worse. We became separated, and with my phone out of battery I had no way of finding him. I knew no one. Having acquired a bottle of Jack Daniel's from one of the icy bathtubs I wandered around looking for some form of amusement and came across a rather large bearded man with long red hair and sunglasses, if you don't mind. He looked like he was having fun. We started speaking.

'What are you on?' I asked him.

He looked at me and said earnestly, 'Honest, bruv, you don't want what I'm having.'

It felt like a scene from *Withnail and I*, where Withnail is presented with a similar predicament by drug-dealing Danny. To which he replied, 'I could take double anything you could.' I wasn't quite as forward as Withnail but was up for a challenge nonetheless.

'Okay,' he shrugged. Pulling a little bottle from his pocket, he asked me to hold out my hand. I did and he poured a small drop of liquid onto my wrist. I looked at it blankly.

'Lick it,' he said.

I did and disappeared into the night. Two hours passed and I felt no more tuned than I had on arrival. I had found Proudlock by now and was telling him about my encounter with the bearded man. Proudlock had limited interest in my story as the stuff hadn't appeared to do anything. Then all of a sudden I spotted the man in question by one of the large outdoor, all-weather speakers. I strolled over to him and informed him that his liquid didn't work. He said that in many cases that was perfectly normal and invited me to have another drop if I so dared. I often have trouble hitting the brakes and in this case obliged him, holding my wrist out again. He chuckled and informed me that I'd be high for the next thirty hours or so. This wasn't particularly amusing as we had been invited to have lunch the following day with Oliver's mother. However, I assumed he was joking and asked him what the substance was.

'It's liquid acid,' he replied.

'I see,' I said. I'd heard of acid and what it does to people and to be honest part of me was very curious. I'd never believed much in hallucinations, having always just assumed they were small splashes of colour or something of equal innocence. I was very much mistaken.

I made the short walk back over to Proudlock and told him that I'd just double-dropped acid. Another forty-five minutes went by and still nothing. We were sitting on top of a haystack, quite a high one, when out of nowhere a metaphorical train hit me. I fell off the haystack onto my back and felt absolutely nothing. It had got me. I felt possessed, as all the clouds in the sky began to swirl into a collective, almost perfectly symmetrical whirlwind, creating a gaping black hole directly above me. It was beautiful and intriguing but this was only the beginning.

When I eventually sat up there was a guy roughly the same age as me who wouldn't break his gaze from mine. He seemed aggressive but I was too high to engage him. He came over and started hurling abuse at me. I felt slightly more in the room at this point so stood up to confront him and rather a large fight broke out. We ended up on the ground, both giving everything we had. I felt like an animal, and was properly laying into him, when suddenly Proudlock grabbed my arm and pinned me to the ground. Everyone was staring at me. It was as if the music had stopped and the atmosphere had completely changed. To my great surprise he asked me what the hell I was doing. I was startled, in a world of my own, looking left and right, trying to figure out where my unreasonable attacker had gone, but there was no one. It was just me. And Proudlock. And an audience.

I'd been fighting a figment of my imagination. What made everything scarier was that I could feel the man's body; I could feel skin, the impact of his fists hitting my face. It was as real as it gets. I'd like to say that was all for the night's festivities but unfortunately this was not so.

My mind went into overload. What's real, what's not? Is Proudlock real? How do I know anything is real now? Hideous question after hideous question flooded through me. Proudlock brought over a cold beer and sat with me for a while as I attempted to allow the drug to blow over. Yet again, wishful thinking. One thing I knew was that I couldn't lose him. He was to be my rock, my base. I was in his hands.

Then a rather attractive blonde girl came and sat near us. I wasn't in the mood to flirt with anyone, but I thought that my head might be in a place whereby I could at least have a conversation with someone, and feeling slightly guilty that I was holding Ollie back from one of his preferred parties, told him to head off and have fun – which he did. I got talking to this girl who seemed very interesting and I thought that the storm may just have been weathered. My mind wasn't capsizing quite so much. I was mid-sentence when Proudlock came back and completely interrupted me.

'Who are you talking to, bro?'

He must have been joking. I turned to look at him, trying to muster a smile.

'Who are you talking to, bro?' he asked again.

My attention turned back towards the girl. I was thinking that if she wasn't there then we had a serious problem. Of course, she didn't exist either. I suppose this was no great surprise but at the time I can assure you that the fear was kicking in. Surely I couldn't have thirty hours of this? I needed the bearded man. At this point I would have settled for anyone who could give me some advice. In the end, there was nothing to do but accept my own stupidity for double-dropping acid, proffered by a stranger at a rave, and wait it out. And hope it didn't stick.

Since that evening I have looked into the effects of what acid can do to an individual and in some more serious cases it can stay with you for life, from one single drop. I've even heard about the philosopher in California who, with his friends, was commissioned by the US Government to trial whether or not the heightened level of activity in a mind influenced by acid might be modified and used in some way to enhance the performance of soldiers in certain conditions. He ended up seeing lobsters in the street.

This information did not surprise me. Perhaps it would have been more useful to have had an education in acid before having tried it.

Hours passed, probably sitting in the same spot. When the time came to leave, it was like being invited to leave hell. But unfortunately a change in location didn't mean that the effects of the drug were left behind. They followed me right into the taxi in the form of gushing water. Proudlock had to deal with me drowning in the back seat for forty minutes or so. I even tried paying the taxi driver to stop the water – he thought I was mad.

Proudlock's mother's house was almost worse than the field. The list is endless: instead of the dog, I got a lion, the portraits were all turning and talking to me, it was Fear and Loathing in the West Country. The only move was to sleep it off. I got into bed feeling unusual but soon found myself drifting off. I knew that sleep would bring peace of mind, and I awoke the following day feeling refreshed. The craziness had stopped, everything seemed normal. I even had a conversation with one of Ollie's friends Paddy, recounting the events of the night before. I was grateful to be sane again.

Ollie's mother's house is beautiful, with a grand staircase that runs directly from ground level up through all the floors right to the top of the house. I was extremely hungry and was heading down to the kitchen to make myself some breakfast when I crossed Ollie's mother on the staircase. We chatted briefly and I explained that things had possibly been taken a little too far the night before, to which she chuckled in her usual friendly way and carried on up the stairs. As I rounded the bend into the kitchen I bumped into Ollie's mum preparing breakfast for the boys. One of them was not real. I dropped to my knees and burst into tears, certain that I was now a schizophrenic. I felt miserable and would have done anything in the world to take back those two little drops on my wrist but the past cannot be reversed and I knew my life was altered forever.

People spent the majority of that day reassuring me they were real but that's what I would expect them to do. I trusted no one. Part of me thought that I should perhaps learn to live with it so I accompanied the boys to Waitrose. This was a shocking idea. There were Babybels the size of the haystacks we'd been sitting on the night before and the place was absolutely rammed with people. Or was it? Who's to know?

Eventually we got back to the house, and I began to see the positives of my newfound imagination as we started to play video games. But during half-time of the first match – which I had only been spectating – things suddenly stopped. It was almost as if there had been a loud noise in my head, which I only noticed once it had disappeared.

'It's gone,' I said.

'It'll be back,' Proudlock replied reassuringly.

'No, mate, it's gone, I know it has.'

I can safely say that everyone I've met since then is real. Although I'm not writing this book to preach, I will allow myself this. If I were you, I would stay well away from acid as it is dangerous, twisted and dark. Being in control is key. Being played like a puppet by your own mind is frightening.

CHAPTER 13

Persistence is Key

It was during my last year at Eton that I met Catherine Dunlop – Caggie – although I'd been smitten by her for many months already, ever since I'd seen her picture on a mate's Facebook page. She was everything I'd ever looked for in a girl: gorgeous face, wavy blonde hair, full lips . . . She was a naturally very beautiful girl, an English rose, and I wanted to meet her. We were introduced by a mutual friend, Milo Osbourne, during a lazy Sunday afternoon at The Builders Arms, just off Sydney Street in Chelsea. Caggie was sitting at a table with friends and she looked amazing. In fact, she looked even more striking than in her pictures. I fell in love on the spot. At moments like these, my advice to be confident and comfortable in one's skin isn't that easy to follow. When you want something this badly, of course there's going to be some fear of rejection. Caggie was not any ordinary girl.

Milo had a sort of brother/sister relationship with her which I hoped would come in handy, but it's impossible to uncook something that is overcooked. Caggie could tell you first-hand that I'm not one to hold back, being a pretty straightforward, straight-talking kind of person. She was not quite ready for the degree of certainty in my declaration that one day we would be married. Not within moments of Milo introducing us anyway. I think I'm right in saying that now she finds it amusing when we look back at it but at the time it was perhaps a little much.

Caggie, like many people, including myself, does not like being told what to do. She takes this to a whole new level by literally doing the opposite most of the time. She didn't understand then – and never has – the fact that my feelings for her were the most genuine I've ever had for a woman. She must have thought I was joking. By then I had developed a bit of a reputation for not being overly serious when it came to commitment and I had also slept with a number of her friends. This rarely helps.

Anyway, after some conversation, Caggie agreed to come on a date with me. Whether she knew it was a date or not, I'm not quite sure; I didn't even ask if she was seeing anyone. I figured that treading lightly around this matter was the best way forward. I say treading lightly because I was on thin ice and wanted to remain above water on this one. No room for mistakes. I had to be with her. She was the only thing missing from my life. The problem with going about things in such an uncompromising way is that you are under constant pressure to perform. I didn't feel like myself around her at the beginning; it was like she had – and to a certain extent still does have – a spell on me. Part of me will always wonder if the future could have been different had I played things a little differently.

I wanted to treat Caggie to the best of everything, and I remember arranging a lovely date to the theatre followed by supper at what has now become my favourite restaurant, Zuma. I spent every penny I had on taking her out, and wasn't sure my card would go through when it came to pay. If only I had taken the time to get to know her better, I would have realized that material things are the last thing on Caggie's mind, and in retrospect, she would have preferred something far more low key. Double fail. Skint with a not-so impressed prospective girlfriend.

I had missed the mark on this one and could tell that she wasn't much interested. Some girls need the security and confidence boost that compliments and kindness can offer but some lean the other way. I was too keen and would have done anything for her – she knew this and found it unattractive. I'm not one for games, and perhaps neither is she, but she was coming off like a pro and I was just lost and in love.

It was a non-starter. We saw each other socially, occasionally we'd have lunch or dinner together, but it never felt like it was going anywhere – not for her anyway. We had drifted into the uncomfortable arena of friendship. She would date other people around me, as I would around her, but I'd always keep my eye on the final prize. This went on for years but whenever I would successfully shift my attention elsewhere, she would reappear on the scene as if on purpose, with a look or a smile or even a rare kiss that would just spiral me straight back to the starting line. I've never been played by a girl before. I'm not saying Caggie was toying with me but that's what it felt like.

Life in the sixth form at Eton continued in the same way, although we were handed the odd interlude to keep us going, such as the chance to spend a month in northern Italy in a place called Imperia, living with Italian families who couldn't speak English. The school thought that we would learn Italian quicker that way and, sure enough, I picked up a good basic understanding of the language that still helps me to get by today. I was staying with a student called Luca who looked like a great big bear and was an excellent tour guide. He had an appetite for drinking and for good Italian grub – both of which were fine by me.

Also, the school hoped to open our eyes to life's opportunities by organizing regular talks given by various inspirational figures. They could be anyone, and in our case included Stelios Haji-Ioannou, who founded easyJet, and adventurer and television presenter Bear Grylls. Bear was a good speaker, and a much admired adventurer, rather like my brother Mike. While Mike had been the youngest Brit to reach the summit of Mount Everest, Bear, who is one year older, had climbed it shortly after him and held the record for the youngest Brit to have summited and returned. After his talk, I spoke to him about my brother. Bear was lovely and had in fact already mentioned

Mike in his autobiography *Facing Up*, which describes his own climb to the top of the world.

Eton has always had a variety of interesting extra-curricular talks and discussions to attend, always something new to learn. Even with these distractions, I couldn't avoid the need to think about the future. As final exams approached, the question of what to do after Eton started to hang over all of us leavers. Film has always been a passion of mine. Having spent years studying acting at Eton and having played a number of roles in various productions, I was deeply intrigued by method actors such as Daniel Day-Lewis and Christian Bale. I would read interviews with these actors after every film they made, wondering how they could spend so long in the frame of mind of such disturbing characters, and we spent a large portion of our final year studying Stanislavsky's methods – the origin of method acting. Eddie Redmayne had left Eton the year I arrived, and since then I have really enjoyed watching his career develop. He really is a fine actor and hopefully one day he will be recognized by the Academy.

I decided the best way to pursue my dream of a film career was to apply to a US college with a good cinema and television department. As it happened, the University of Southern California on the outskirts of Hollywood was unsurpassed in reputation. It was here that many of film's most successful directors and screenwriters, and indeed actors, learned their craft, including George Lucas and Ron Howard. One of my favourite comedy geniuses, Will Ferrell, also went to USC, to study sports broadcasting.

So, having spoken with the family, I applied for a place at the University of Southern California. It would be the only university that I applied to in the end. I didn't want a safety net. I took a sort of flip-a-coin approach – if I got in I would go, if I didn't I would start grafting somewhere. University is considered by many families, especially Americans, to be extremely important for future career options – which is, of course, sensible. My view, probably inherited from The Band, is that one's occupation or career path depends largely on personal character and whether or not you can actually do the job. Can you sell or market or invent something or can't you? Like so many students, I wasted time at university – time that could have been better spent networking and getting my feet in doors. It seems that, for some, university is a less regimented version of school, with better nightlife and fewer rules. The Band is a believer in education and didn't discourage me from going to university. Whether or not he believes certain university courses to be education, strictly speaking, is another matter. Medicine, sure. Acting, perhaps not.

I received the news that I had been accepted into USC's Cinema Television Programme for a Bachelor of Arts degree in early 2006. Now I just had to pass my A-levels. As the exams approached, I went into cramming mode, helped yet again by my friend Mazdak. We achieved three As. These grades were not predicted and although the school must have been happy with the results, I'm sure many of the teachers felt they were undeserved. Mazdak was always there for me in my moments of need and I will forever be grateful to him for being such a good friend.

Although excited about the move to California, I was also sad to leave Eton. I'd loved my time there; not only had I made lifelong friends but the place itself had given me so much. The traditions, the theatre, the facilities, the sports, the art schools, the staff, the culture, all are fantastic. If I'm ever fortunate enough to have a son, and the means to send him to Eton, I definitely will – and I trust they'd be kind enough to take him.

CHAPTER 14

Frat Boy

One of the first things I became interested in on arrival at the University of Southern California was the American fraternity system. I'd heard many urban legends about the pledging process, and having enjoyed movies such as *Old School* and *Animal House*, I appreciated the hilarity of these almost cult-like brotherhoods. At no point was I looking to take it seriously, nor was I ever going to have any real respect for it, but I certainly couldn't ignore my curiosity.

During the first week of the American university system it is possible to 'rush' fraternities and sororities. Rush week is a complete joke. Each house throws a party of astronomical proportions every night for seven days. At USC all of the houses, both frats and sororities, are on the same street, the actual name of which escapes me but which was appropriately called Frat Row. It was like being a child at a zoo without supervision – ambulances, police every night, girls pepper-spraying people, sex in public, you name it. I loved it.

As it happens, the person I was sharing a room with in the halls, Alex Fine, turned out to be a really exceptional guy. One night, whilst wading through the hordes of ruined people we came across two typically American cheerleaders. We had a few drinks and during the conversation Alex jokingly threw in that I was a virgin. Before I had time to object, I couldn't help but notice that the level of interest towards me from both girls had risen quite drastically so I ran with it. As it turned out, being a curious British virgin who's saving his first time for someone really special flew particularly well with the American crowd. This later became something of a theme, a rather genius one at that. Occasionally, a girl would offer to teach me a thing or two so I wouldn't embarrass myself in front of the love of my life – and I'd often accept. It was only when a few of these willing teachers were in the same room that my cover would be blown.

The point of these parties was for each house to appeal to the new students. Every house has its own attributes – some attract athletes, some attract musicians. Delta Chi seemed to attract characters, which is why I chose it, and they liked the idea of having a Brit join their fraternity.

Once you've chosen your preferred house, they must in turn choose you. Assuming they do and a bond has been created, you then become a pledge for that house. In my case, the pledging process, with its endless initiation rites, lasted about ten weeks and was pretty draining.

At one point, quite early on, I found myself sitting blindfolded in a basement with the other new pledges, surrounded by crates of beer and listening to the same song playing on repeat extremely loudly. The students who already belonged to the house (active brothers) made it clear that this wouldn't end until we could recite the Greek alphabet one after the other in full. This is particularly difficult when you can't see or hear each other, and there are fourteen of you. The only rule was that we had to be drinking at all times – and this was enforced. If you were caught not sipping your beer every few seconds, you were given a double shot of tequila. Twenty cans of beer and ten shots later, the Greek alphabet was becoming more and more impossible. It took over nine hours to complete the task but to this day I can still rattle off the Greek alphabet at will.

The song, by the way, was the now incredibly irritating 'Bring it' by Cobra Starship from *Snakes on a Plane*. Whenever I hear it now I know how Bradley Cooper's character in *The Silver Linings Playbook* felt when his wedding song played. Fortunately, due to Cobra Starship's lack of popularity, this is not very often.

By the end of the tenth week, after long and rigorous tests of mind and body, we arrived at our final night before becoming actives. We were instructed to put on sports gear as we would be going on a brief run as a group; a lap of the campus as tradition would have it. We were told to meet outside the main door at 10 p.m. Once we were all assembled, we were asked to regroup in the basement.

Something wasn't right, but by now we were very much used to the fact that nothing we heard was true and that we couldn't trust anyone.

The basement was pitch black and silent. When the lights came on, we saw that a boxing ring had been assembled in the centre of the room and a couple of hundred of the finest sorority sisters had accepted the invitation to come to fight night. The pressure was on. Some of us were immediately delighted, some scared. The rules were explained – we were each able to choose, in turn, one active brother to take out any aggression on that may have built up over the previous ten weeks. Many of the pledges had been pushed to breaking point by the active brothers – whose behaviour hadn't been particularly brotherly at the best of times – but now it was our turn.

My fight was brief, mainly due to the fact that I'd developed genuine hatred for my counterpart. Hate's a strong word and I'm not one for disliking anyone but this guy was a particular kind of person. His pathetic attempt to become my friend just before entering the ring fell very much on deaf ears. He was unfit, slow, overweight and would have had trouble running up a flight of stairs but at this point I wasn't feeling sympathetic. Also, I was currently playing inside centre for USC's varsity rugby team and had a crowd to impress. Let's just say that for what he'd put me through over those ten weeks he was lucky to get away with just a broken nose.

To British people, being a frat boy usually sounds unappealing but in many ways it was a memorable time because I shared the experience with Alex and another new friend Max Doyle, two of New Jersey's finest. Max's fight went pretty well too, considering that he went on to practise UFC to quite a high level. These kinds of experiences really do bring you closer together with your peers, and by the end you do feel like brothers.

Unsurprisingly, my preferred route through university was social. The course itself was pretty slow-paced and sugar-coated, covering most aspects of film-making, from cinematography to scriptwriting.

I was in LA for nine months, and had a really fantastic time. The quality of life was higher there than in the UK – everywhere you looked there were girls walking around the place like they'd just stepped off a film set, and every waiter I spoke to was also an actor, or maybe the actors were all waiters. I'm not sure. Everyone was really good-looking but none were quite as beautiful as the one who got away . . .

Before moving into the frat house, I was living with Finey in Pardee Towers on the campus of USC a few doors down from Ashton Palmer. It was another case of love at first sight. Thinking about it, every girl I've ever gone out with has been like that, bar maybe one. The first time I saw Ashton walking along the halls, I knew that I needed her in my life in some way. Friend, girlfriend, godmother to my children with Caggie, whatever. She looked angelic, petite and perfect with vibrant green eyes. As she walked down the long corridor, I tried to figure out what I was going to say to her, but in the end I didn't say a word. A simple hello may have sufficed but the moment came and went in a heartbeat and something stopped me from speaking.

I was captivated by her and the first take began. Given that we were living in the same halls, at least I knew I'd see her again. It wasn't long before the two of us were hanging out fairly regularly. When the words 'my boyfriend' came out of her mouth I had a physical ache in my heart. I had a new enemy and I'd never even met the guy. I was outraged at my own degree of jealousy. Was this guy in a band? Of course he was.

Ashton and I drifted into friendship – and, as with Caggie, this is a dangerous place to be if you like someone. One day I went to 'borrow the next series of *Family Guy*' (or any other excuse to see her) and noticed that she had been crying. We sat on the bed and had a chat and she told me that her boyfriend had broken up with her. As well as feeling sorry for her, I've rarely in my life felt as delighted as I did in that moment. I had to actively refrain from cartwheeling out the door. My life had just become complete. Well, completion seemed imminent but I was unsure how long to leave it before saying something – too long and she might start dating the drummer, too short and she'd think I was insensitive. It had to be just right.

A suitable moment arrived, but I just couldn't find the words. Opportunities came and went. Once we were lying on the bed in my room watching a TV show and, without her noticing, I kept sneaking glances at her. She was so close, it would only take a small move towards her . . .

That fear of rejection was back again and this time it was just too great because if I got it wrong I'd lose her as a friend as well. It's a time I'll always look back on and regret. I should have trusted my heart and instincts and been more of a man. If I'd asked her out and she'd said no, it would have hurt at the time but at least I wouldn't be asking myself questions like 'what if?' all these years down the line.

To this day, Ashton Palmer probably has no idea how I felt about her. When I'm done sending a copy of this book to every Ashton Palmer in the States, perhaps she will.

When I wasn't failing to win Ashton's heart, I hung out with Brody Jenner and Spencer Pratt, the two original cast members of *The Hills*, and a friend of theirs, Stavros Niarchos III. The connection was made through one of Eden Rock's clients, a young man called Jared Najjar. He and his family had just begun to stay at the hotel when I was accepted into USC, and I ended up visiting his house in the Hollywood Hills regularly. Jared is an amazing American guy who has recently developed a liking for England and its culture. He has a profound love of art and is amongst the most eligible guys in Los Angeles. Jared and Brody were inseparable.

I remember at the time being particularly impressed by the way of life Jared and his circle enjoyed. One day I was having lunch with Brody and Stavros who were exchanging opinions about whether or not Stavros's relationship with Paris would continue. It later dawned on me they were talking about Paris Hilton. Perhaps my relationship dilemmas at USC weren't quite the high-end problems I'd thought.

Jared now owns and operates Prism, a particularly successful art gallery and business in LA. Although this is relatively new, Jared has always done well for himself. When I first met him, he had already created a clothing and jewellery line called Archangel and was dripping in his own product. He loved diamonds and gold and expensive watches and had a general flair for what some people perceive to be the finer things in life. For a young kid who didn't know LA, Jared was It. He had Rolls-Royces, Ferraris, Mercs and Astons all parked in a row outside his house in the Hollywood Hills. Popular stars like Brody and Spencer came round, whilst about ten gorgeous girls from different modelling houses would be relaxing in or around the infinity pool most days.

Jared lived a carefree life which was kind of how I'd envisioned USC to be. I almost began to work a bit for Jared, picking up merchandise from factories and delivering it to shops with the help of his best friend at the time, and my close friend to date, Taylor Mosher, still known to the LA public as Sleazy T. I wasn't an employee of the company and didn't get paid, but in return for helping out, my expenses would be covered while with the boys. And if I wanted to take a girl on an expensive date, say, Jared would slip me a card. It was a good team.

I guess the company that would closest compare to Archangel, as it's no longer around, would be Chrome

Hearts, also LA-based. Archangel jewellery took a specific person to pull it off, and it could be seen to border on the ridiculous in the eyes of the more modest, quiet individual. Archangel never used anything other than precious stones and metals, the cheapest of which were black diamonds and silver. I felt like part of the company now, and Jared would let me wear anything from the lines on our nights out in LA. These included heavy rose-gold chains, with large crosses of the same material peppered with precious stones. At the time I was most attracted to the larger rose-gold pieces, mainly because of their aesthetic beauty, but I could never bring myself to leave the house in them. I'd like to say it was for fear of losing them, although it's probably because I knew I couldn't pull them off. Also, I doubt that Jared would have been keen to pay for the amount of therapeutic massages I'd need if I was to walk around in those heavy chains all day long. They were a display of wealth, and although they were things of beauty, they were not elegant. Some of them would fetch six figures. I would usually go for the silver wings, one of which had thirteen small black diamonds lining the edge, and perhaps a couple of rings and a bracelet or two. Elegant, understated – just about.

Looking back at all of this now, my time in LA with these boys may well have been the best of my life. I don't consider myself to be a particularly materialistic kind of guy, but when it's all on tap it is nice.

If you're a fan of *The Hills* you may have noticed a fair few of the cast sporting Archangel gear, particularly

Spencer and Brody. Brody and I clicked instantly – when Jared was busy we'd often spend time together. Brody was a nice guy with a good heart, something that can't be said for everyone in his position. At the time *The Hills* was a powerhouse. We would be followed by paps and even when we would hop in cars to change location they would take to their bikes and relocate right along with us. Brody had very limited privacy but he dealt with it well. He was polite to journalists and photographers and they respected him for that.

One night later that year, we all got together and went out for a nice meal at Koi's on La Cienega Boulevard. I hadn't seen the boys in a few weeks, as with exams and other college requirements it was difficult to get away. Brody had started dating Avril Lavigne, or was just about to, one of the two – I can't be sure whether or not they arrived together but they seemed pretty comfortable. Jared, Taylor, some girls and a few other characters were there. It was a table of about ten and in their usual expansive manner, there was no holding back on the ordering. Expensive bottles of champagne, saki and vodka kept arriving during dinner and what could only be described as most of the menu turned up too. The bill was between four and five grand. If we had split it ten ways, my card would have been declined.

The time came to pay and I was getting a little perturbed over how to have a quiet word with Jared without drawing too much attention to the fact that my rather ordinary debit card might not be able to withstand the strain of its imminent beating. Just as I was about to catch Jared's eye, he announced that we should play card roulette. I had never heard of card roulette but I could only assume that one poor person was going to have to pick up the bill and with ten to one odds I fancied my chances.

'Only the guys,' Jared yelled. Although it is the gentlemanly thing to do, I did find it a little ironic in this case as Avril Lavigne and the somewhat recognizable models were all considerably richer than me.

Four to one. Not so good. So I had a 75 per cent chance of getting away with this but it would be just my luck to get stuck with this bill. Perhaps I could give Jared one of those rings back.

We each handed our cards to Avril, two black, one dusty and one with holes in it. She shuffled them under the table, then threw one into the centre of the table. My heart stopped – call an ambulance. My card was staring at me as cheers erupted from the rest of the crew. I was the only person not laughing, and I felt my world begin to run in slow motion as I had to think how to pay this gigantic bill. Do I give it to the waiter and sign and hope for the best? Do I pretend to have just bought a car? Or do I just look genuinely surprised when the card bounces. After all, I did want to be an actor. All of these thoughts ran through my head in a split second. I took a deep breath and opened my mouth to say something – anything – when Jared shouted, 'Next card! Topper's out.'

Topper was a nickname given to me by the boys during

my time spent with them in LA. I'm not quite sure why but I liked it. It sounded cool with an American twang.

Much like the relief when the pro left the room in Johannesburg, I felt free again. Not only had we just had the most incredible dinner, it was once again on the house. But this time I didn't have to feel guilty about it because I'd agreed to play card roulette. Two more cards fell and Taylor was left with the bill. I did feel slightly sorry for him as Jared and Brody were in a far better position to pay, but Taylor shouldn't have played if he didn't have the funds!

But LA life wasn't all about partying and girls; I was also serious about trying to make it as an actor.

Now, I was lucky enough to have one or two friends in high places. Howard Gittis was a major player in Hollywood and a director on the boards of various companies including Panavision Inc. and Revlon. I knew him from St Barths, where he used to holiday with his wonderful wife. Howard said he saw something in me, and when I arrived in LA he introduced me to people. I am grateful to him for that.

I can't remember specifically what the movie was called, or if it was actually made, but Howard helped me to get my first audition. I was familiar with stage work and acting but had never done anything to camera before. It was a beautiful day in LA, as always, when I began to climb the stairs to audition room B in what appeared to be a shady apartment block downtown somewhere. It became clear I was in the right place when, at the top of the stairs, I was met by fifteen or so young men who were not too dissimilar to myself and all within a few years of each other. This was for a seemingly random role in a Christmas movie but some people were taking it quite seriously. At the time I thought this kind of role was simply given to people through word of mouth but apparently auditioning was to be far more competitive than I had originally perceived. I was nervous when I read for the part but I suppose that's normal. They asked me to play a sixteen-year-old, not the kind pretending to be in medical school as I was when I was sixteen, but an actual sixteen-year-old of which I had not much experience.

The audition seemed to run smoothly but I didn't get the part. It was thought that I looked too old to play a sixteen-year-old. In fact, they thought I looked to be more in my early twenties. Can't people just be whatever age they are? Not in Hollywood. But I understood where they were coming from and knew that hundreds of young actors try out for a handful of roles every day. It was good to have experienced a real audition.

As my first year at USC drew to an end, I was having second thoughts about film school. I'd developed a desire to make my own money – a characteristic The Band developed at a young age too – and another three years at film school and more failed auditions would mean that I wasn't going to be able to fund the lifestyle I'd become accustomed to. I wasn't giving up on acting and I still wanted to pursue a career in film or TV one day, but there were a couple of other issues influencing my decision, too. The education at USC was a bit soft. One of my classes – and this was not optional – was titled Love, Marriage and the Experience of Being a Wife, something I'd hoped never to be. Granted, I did arrive slightly too late to sign up for the other courses that I would have found arguably more interesting but this course was made a requirement nonetheless. There was one other guy in this class – he too had figured out the silver lining in the form of the heavily tilted ratio of female to male students. We ended up sitting next to each other most classes and by the end of the year had extremely high ideas of what to expect from a future spouse.

The American university system can also be a bit of a nightmare because every piece of allocated work counts towards a final grade at the end of the year. Some of these pieces can make up as much as a third of your grade and obviously these are taken quite seriously. But all the minor essays, etc., that students such as myself frequently ignored, could drag down your average to a point where it's impossible to pass the course. In other words, every piece of work must be completed and on time. It was difficult to care about deadlines when faced with so many pleasurable distractions. Matt Jurow, a friend from Delta Chi, and I would often go and surf in the morning before classes and then come the afternoon we'd enjoy a few drinks on the outskirts of the campus in 35-degree heat, surrounded by cool interesting people. It was hard to break the mould and sit indoors and work. My usual cramming techniques at the end of the year were irrelevant at this college. Even if a student gets 100 per cent on their mid-term and final exam, demonstrating that they have understood the course in full, they still need to have completed the rest of the work to pass the year.

It's no secret that colleges such as these are also expensive to attend and I couldn't help but think that The Band's hard-earned cash wasn't being used particularly well out there. It was arguably the best time of my life but I couldn't justify doing it for three more years. A bachelor of arts degree in cinema and television would in the eyes of many make no difference to the outcome of my acting career, or any other career for that matter. Also it would be nice to get back to see the family and close friends at home.

It was time for a re-think and I set off to make some money.

CHAPTER 15

The Terrorist's Son

We chatted a lot as a family about what I should do next and Mum and Dad advised against entering any of the businesses in which Dad was invested, at least for the time being. Instead, they counselled me to make my own way in life and to find out what would best suit my particular nature. They said there was lots of time and the choice was mine. Good advice, I thought. They also suggested that in the meantime a period of hands-on work would be useful and they hoped that the discipline involved in having to work every day might hit the mark with me. The hotel in St Barths was growing quickly at that time and fitted the bill perfectly – and I was happy to agree.

So it was back to St Barths for me but this time in a more serious way. The Band was to oversee what we had agreed would be nine months of work experience, with the aim that I would learn something of the ropes in as many jobs in the hospitality sector as possible. So I did a month each of chauffeuring, bartending, working in the kitchen, as a maid, on the reception desk . . . you name it, I did it. It would all be useful and I was learning practical skills that I hoped would come in handy wherever my eventual career path led – and so it proved to be.

Eden Rock had developed a lot by this stage and about twenty-four houses had been built on the beach. My parents had expanded by buying an old hotel adjacent to Eden Rock and all of the space it occupied. Once building work was complete, the complex included the spectacular new house 'Villa Rockstar' which was about 16,000 square feet in size and included two pools, a bar, a gym, a communications centre, a screening room and a professional recording studio containing, amongst other gear, the console John Lennon had used when he recorded 'Imagine'. Really iconic stuff and Beatles fans continue to visit to view and pat it to this day.

Also, Mum had been working to introduce art as an integral part of the resort. There was now a gallery and all hotel rooms contained some original artwork. The artist-in-residence programme had been established and Eden Rock was working with the New York Academy of Art, whose management sent artists to St Barths who may not have sold or even exhibited before. They stayed at Eden Rock free of charge and were encouraged to create art and exhibit it however they wished, hopefully deriving some inspiration from the vivid tropical colours and the desert island feel. The artists gave lessons to children and were urged to chat to guests about their work, with a view to attracting commissions and the ability to earn a livelihood from their art. About ten resident artists per year are sponsored in this way by Eden Rock and the New York Academy.

A favourite celebrity visited the hotel during my time working there. I was reading *Scar Tissue* by Anthony Kiedis, the lead singer of the Red Hot Chili Peppers, and was engrossed in the high-octane hedonism that had filled his life, the details of which just flowed off the pages and were almost beyond belief. Amazingly, no sooner had I finished the last sentence, put down the book and sat back to reflect on what had happened to him than I saw the man himself sitting in the restaurant. I went over to talk to him and he was happy to sign my book. He was just as I'd envisioned he would be, cool, calm, collected.

This sort of thing happens almost on a daily basis in St Barths. Every evening, when the heat came off a bit and the sun was starting to go down, I'd run on the beach or the sports track, which had been generously provided by Roman Abramovich. I was probably in the best physical condition of my life at this point but that didn't mean that my downtime was spent being sensible. The social scene always was, and always will be, one of the greatest things about the island. Outdoor drinks in the evening, with the fun atmosphere that seems to prevail over there, were a definite highlight of the day.

Given that I was doing all this running I wanted something to strive towards so signed up to do my first New York Marathon. When training for an event such as a marathon it's fairly normal for a person to stop drinking or at least to moderate one's alcohol intake a few months prior to the event. I approached my first marathon in a sensible manner by taking it pretty easy on the drink and training hard. Such a regime means that when you drink properly again, the effects seem to hit you in a more dramatic way. This was certainly true of the night I am about to describe, although I would later find out that my state was helped along by a certain dark character.

I had never thought that The Feeling nightclub was inappropriately or ironically named until this particular evening. Despite the fact that I'd ended up in the establishment, I hadn't had a single drink. It will come as no surprise to you that late-night clubs can be a little boring when not intoxicated, so I allowed myself the pleasure of just the one. As I waited to be served, I couldn't help but notice that on the other side of the room there was a rather strange figure whose gaze seemed fixed on me. He was a skinny, much older man with bleached white hair, gold earrings and a sleeveless denim jacket. I've never been homophobic and have many gay friends, but this man was unnerving. I tried my best not to look at him but found myself constantly checking if he was still there. Sometimes he'd disappear from view, only to return moments later always looking at me. Before I knew it he was standing next to me at the bar, striking up a conversation. He had very little respect for my personal space, and it was generally uncomfortable being around him. I moved to join some friends on a nearby table, trying not to make a meal of it.

As my vodka went down I started to feel unusually light-headed and needed fresh air badly. In the back of my mind I knew I'd only had one drink so I just decided to sit it out and wait to feel better. The effects of the alcohol soon began to feel like too much to handle, though. I was beginning to think that I'd become ill when I suddenly looked up and saw that the man's cold gaze had turned into a suggestive smile. It was then that I suspected he might have spiked my drink, and realizing that I needed to get out of there, I made my excuses and left. I only lived down the road and still felt that I had the capacity to make it home without ringing any alarm bells. So, dropping a few notes on the table, I wandered out of the front door.

The fresh air helped a little but it had become clear to me by then that this feeling was not being caused by the drink; there was something else coursing through my system, something stronger. The drug was really beginning to take effect. I felt slower, nauseous and in need of rest. I'd barely made it round the corner when my only option was to stop and sit on a nearby rock in the hope of it passing. I was awake and alert but my body was numb. I tried to shout to the bouncers for help but couldn't – the muscles in my neck were also anaesthetized. I was helpless, an easy target for the man, who had of course been watching his imminent victim's every move and was not far behind me. He approached and, in the knowledge that I was unable to move or speak, pretended to know me and tried to look after me. Being conscious, hearing this was terrifying. People were walking past asking if I needed anything and he would simply reply that he was taking care of me and that we were friends, and not to worry.

When there was no one around he'd run his fingers through my hair and whisper to me that everything was going to be okay. I felt like a fly trapped in a spider's web. Finally, my eyes began to close as I succumbed to the drowsiness. The last thoughts running through my mind before slipping into unconsciousness were: What did this man want with me? More than anything it was likely to be of a sexual nature, but what if I woke up in a bathtub without a kidney? What if I didn't wake up at all?

I will always be thankful that the man in question was not physically strong. In fact, he was bony and weak. In order not to draw any attention to his sick plan he would need to move me on his own, and dead weight is pretty hard to shift, especially *my* dead weight, which was still considerable despite the marathon training. The next thing I remember is being dragged, his hands under my armpits, into his car, which he had brought round to the other side of the club by this point. The noise of the car and the general discomfort of being dragged brought me back slightly. Without making him aware that I was semi-conscious I tried to move my fingers and toes, which I could, sort of. I tried to open and close my mouth and to my relief I could do that too. Sensing this would be my only chance to get out of this vile person's clasp, I suddenly began moving and making as much noise as possible, hoping desperately that someone would notice. It was getting light by now.

He tried to cover my mouth with his hand but I

responded by trying to bite him, and thankfully the struggle did attract one passer-by's attention, who in turn alerted the doorman and my good friend, Hervé. Having taught tae kwon do to a number of local children, including me a few years prior to this, Hervé was generally a man not to be messed with. When I saw him round the corner I don't believe I've ever been so happy. The relief was so great that I passed out immediately and didn't even get to see the conclusion of the night's festivities. When I came to, Hervé assured me that the man certainly wouldn't be returning to St Barths any time soon. I have to say this particular news didn't bother me at all. The drug did eventually wear off and much to my delight, my organs are still intact.

I was back to full physical fitness by October. I was doing the marathon with James and some people we knew from London. We took a long weekend off work and went to NYC. The marathon usually takes place during the first weekend of November, which sometimes happens to coincide with Halloween. New York Halloween parties are exceptional and in no circumstances to be missed, not even if they fall the night before marathon day. As it did in 2007.

We were all happy to have one or two drinks during the nights leading up to the weekend, with a view to taking it easy on Saturday. Unfortunately, one particular friend (who shall remain nameless) and I couldn't quite help ourselves when we heard about certain not-to-be-ignored parties happening on the Saturday. All self-regulation went out the window and we barely made it back to the hotel in time to catch the bus taking us to the start line. We even had a beer in the room as we picked up our trainers. Being fairly fit at the time, we didn't think it would matter.

I have to say that the first few miles would probably have been easier without a bottle of whisky coursing through my veins but we pushed through nonetheless. To make things worse we were in separate starting groups. We must have been the only two drunk runners of the tens of thousands participating but at least we were in high spirits. Although we didn't see each other during the entire race, we somehow managed to finish a minute apart, which is a bizarre coincidence that could not be repeated.

My friend was waiting at the finish line for ten minutes or so by the time I arrived, but fate would have it that I'd crossed the starting line eleven minutes after him, therefore beating him by fifty odd seconds. To make matters worse for him, the general saying in marathons is that anything under four hours is a good time. I was just under, he was just over. Better luck next time.

The heat on St Barths seems to encourage people to become more easy-going and the beauty of the island and the holiday vibe make for inevitable short-term romances, even for those who aren't on holiday. That year in particular was host to a few of my more disturbing experiences, some of which I'll share with you.

One evening I came across a rather interesting bunch of Canadians. What they were on I'm not quite sure but no questions were asked. I'd learned my lesson by then. There were three girls and two guys, one of whom was called Ben. The girls were beautiful, and I enjoyed talking to them. The whole group had a very odd dynamic to it, and one person's relationship with another wasn't particularly clear. The girls were forward and flirty and the guys were either slightly oblivious to it or simply didn't mind. Despite the fact that Ben seemed open to the point of arrogance about the girls being interested in other guys, he definitely ran the show. He was a man of few words but a total character.

When someone suggested that we have an afterparty, I wasn't quite sure where to go as I didn't have my usual holiday room or any special privileges now I was working. Spencer's Cabin was too small and the staffroom, positioned just off the hotel, wasn't much better. The only thing that this group seemed concerned about was the size of the bed. I explained my room could probably fit six people and Ben and I understood each other, perhaps a little too well.

Things didn't take long to escalate once we arrived back at the room. Unable to use room service as an employee, I disappeared off to grab a few bottles. I was only gone five minutes but by the time I got back there was limited interest in the alcohol. I was invited to get involved which I did without hesitation. The three girls were exceptional and we hooked up with one another in turn. We were all busy at all times but the night took a slightly odd turn when Ben decided to multi-task. There was multi-tasking going on by default anyway but we'd kept it straight until this point.

Ben isn't gay, he's not even bisexual, but on this particular occasion he did become a little over-familiar. I was engaged in an activity that had impaired my vision and whilst I was enjoying a hand job from what I hoped was one of the nifty Canadian girls, I couldn't help but notice a slightly firmer grip than had been the case earlier that evening.

'Ben,' I said, 'stick to the girls, mate. Not my thing.'

He understood and things carried on as normal. People finished and/or became tired and gradually the numbers in the bed decreased. Drinks were poured as the group sex fizzled out until we were all just chilling. I liked my new Canadian friends and their free-spirited attitude. Ben and I just carried on talking as before. Things weren't even particularly awkward – I just completely let it slide as if to suggest sixsomes were a fairly usual occurrence.

I had always found older women attractive. Perhaps this was subconsciously because I knew it would be just sex to them and that's all I wanted at the time. On one occasion I found myself attracted to a woman who described herself as being in her mid-forties – I'd say mid-fifties but it didn't matter to me. There was something about her; she seemed powerful and charismatic. We met in town and hit it off immediately. Another thing that I find enticing about older women is that they have a firmer understanding of men. For this short period in my life there were no games, only limited flirting and no fear of rejection. The nights we'd go back to her villa weren't meaningful; they were just fun for an eighteen-year-old at the time.

Older women became something of the norm for a while. I liked the fact that commitment wasn't even a possibility. One evening my mother was having a dinner party and had invited some women she knew from the island. Whether or not you could class these women as my mother's friends is up for discussion but I didn't think she would mind if I came along and had a harmless look around. Halfway through dinner, and much like that famous moment in *Wedding Crashers*, I felt a foot on my thigh under the table. I wasn't quite sure who it was given that both women opposite me were engaged in conversation but I quite fancied one of them. Thankfully, after locking eyes for a moment, it became obvious it was the right one, and after dinner we became far better acquainted.

Of the many jobs I did whilst at Eden Rock, bartending was my favourite. Few places in the world are more enjoyable to sip a cocktail at than Eden Rock's On the Rocks bar looking out over one of St Barths' most beautiful bays and the sea surrounding it. The place is constantly teeming with characters, from Hollywood A-listers to war veterans. It is the place to be. As well as being a beehive of social activity, the bar has a long and interesting cocktail list. I would spend hours learning how to perfect the drinks that I and so many others have enjoyed, and even helped create Eden Rock's chocolate orange martini and their passion fruit zest mojito. All the guests visit the bar at some point so it's arguably the best place in the hotel to get to know them. And everyone needs the barman onside so I was always in a fairly strong position when it came to asking questions of our many interesting clients.

Despite being the owner's son, I was asked by senior management not to be over-familiar with the guests – something I always found difficult but agreed was the correct call. Every night, women would sit at the bar and chat to me, sometimes opening up about their secrets and occasionally their problems. It's funny how alcohol and a barman can encourage women to bare their souls. Some of these ladies would be single, some not, but most had something they wanted to talk about. I would listen and try to be understanding and honest.

It was while working the bar that I experienced what was to become quite a strange escapade. An unusually attractive middle-aged couple came to the bar for some drinks before going out into town. They seemed lovely and engaged me in conversation fairly early on. Although I was serving many other people at the time, we kept a conversation going between the three of us for about an hour or so. They weren't talking to any other guests or even each other for that matter – it was as if the three of us were all out together despite the fact that I was working. I didn't find this strange at the time because they had probably spent all day in each other's company and no doubt fancied a chat with someone else. I really respected him; he was cool in his own right and seemed extremely comfortable with life. Although she was stunning, I didn't see her as someone that I would even try and sleep with. They seemed happy and in love.

They asked me where the hot spots were in town and how they could get in. By this point we'd become acquainted so I offered to drive them to one once I'd finished work. I was meeting some friends there anyway so it wasn't an imposition. They had a couple more rounds and I joined them for the last one before quickly throwing on a clean shirt and driving us into Gustavia. It was only then that it became apparent they were a rather strange couple. Once we were out of the car and walking towards the entrance to the club, the woman grabbed my hand just to hold it. There were no hills, it hadn't rained and her husband was standing right next to me. Before even having time to react, I realized he had spotted us and was entirely unfazed. He kept walking as if he'd seen this all before and didn't care.

Once in the club advances came regularly from his wife but at no point was she trying to hide it from him. She'd tried to kiss my neck whilst I was ordering a drink for her husband, again right in front of him. I'd heard of open marriages but I always assumed there'd be some degree of secrecy. I began to wonder whether or not he was just turning a blind eye to it because it bothered him or whether he genuinely didn't care. Turns out the blind eye wasn't so blind as he turned to me and said, 'My wife wants to have sex with you and I want to watch.'

This offer was quite unusual, like many of the offers received on St Barths. Whether or not you decide to take people up on them is entirely your decision . . .

*

Things at the hotel went back to normal and I became the hotel chauffeur for a period. Not as fun as the bar but considered to be the best job. The chauffeur is the first face to greet the clients at the airport and the last person they see as they leave – both moments in which they feel particularly generous, most of the time. Punctuality was the main requirement for the job. You had to be at the airport and at the client's room at a certain time. I'd get my schedule the night before and so could plan my social life far more in advance. Whilst working you were in an air-conditioned people carrier which was nice as the heat regularly hit 33 degrees.

One day I was asked if, in between client arrivals, I could keep my eye open for a young lady called Sophie who had been employed to work the shop. Apparently she was from Sweden and difficult to miss. Whoever told me that was certainly not wrong. Sophie was my age and would later be 'discovered' by Patrick Demarchelier and taken to New York to work as a model. She was truly stunning and had a way about her that made her attractive to all types and ages. Sophie was new to the island and knew only one person, who also worked in the shop, although her natural manner made it easy for her to fit in. We would go out in groups and enjoy ourselves regularly. I was really quite taken by her but figured she must be used to overconfident guys asking her out so took it quite slowly on this occasion. We became friendly and it was obvious that there could be something there, although neither one of us spoke about it for the first few weeks. Although we were drifting into

Eden Rock – St Barths.

With my favourite *American Pie* star, Tara Reid.

The one that got away: Ashton Palmer.

With the parents in St Barths.

A Matthews' family portrait. Mum and I are on the left, my sister Nina and her husband Adam are on the right, and Dad is in the middle with Nina and Adam's four children, Lily, Yasmina, Rosa and Tristan.

Above With Alex Webb in Movida during Veneer days.

Above left With Fred Sundberg and Ollie Proudlock at an exhibition of works by artists mentored by Eric Fischl, the Eden Rock Gallery, 2009.

Left Suited and booted for my first day in the City.

Right The morning after, with Hugo and Prudders – not feeling good.

Out and about with Funda Onal in 2011.

At an event with Louise Thompson in 2012.

On the red carpet with Caggie Dunlop and Millie Mackintosh, shortly after my powerboat accident in April 2012.

Above With Jamie Laing at the launch party for his sweet shop Candy Kittens, August 2012.

Right Riding the waves with Chloe Levitt-Collins during filming for *The Bachelor*.

Left The eventual winner, Khloe Evans. We had fun, but a long-term romance wasn't on the cards for us.

A happy moment with Lucy at the BAFTAs.

Celebrating our win at the BAFTAs, 2013.

Golden!

With my buddy in crime, Stephanie Pratt.

being just good friends, she could tell that I liked her – as could everyone else. Masking feelings has never been a strong point of mine. This was not a Caggie or an Ashton situation because I was going to have to leave the island at the end of the year and I doubted strongly that she'd be moving with me. So although I knew it was risky and work could become awkward, I mustered up the courage to tell her how I felt. It was a risk I was willing to take to make my stay worthwhile.

We started dating and everything was going well. I really felt happy and work had become all the more enjoyable. But as we all know by now, life on St Barths isn't entirely normal and with a girl like this on my arm, trouble was only just around the corner. Colonel Gaddafi's son, with his penchant for young blonde models, was on the island . . .

Sophie and I had enjoyed a lovely dinner in the harbour and were keen to prolong the evening as, by a not so strange coincidence, we were both free the following day. Knowing how to work the system has its benefits. We were sitting in a club on top of a hill having had a few drinks when a tall man with long dark hair approached us quite suddenly. He stood directly in front of our table, pointed at Sophie and explained rather bluntly, 'I will have her in my bed tonight.'

Assuming that this guy was either high or joking, I laughed in his face and told him to try his luck elsewhere. Of course I was much ruder than that, but wouldn't want to offend any of you. But he had made up his mind and didn't respond well to my lack of respect.

'You have no idea who I am, do you?'

'You're someone who is going to get the fuck away from my table.'

We exchanged a cold glare and he pointed a finger in my face then calmly turned around and walked away. I sat back down next to Sophie and made sure she was all right before attempting to proceed with our evening. Just moments later I clocked a group of men, five including the gruff stranger, walking towards our table more hastily than I happened to like. These men were indescribably huge, with no necks, dressed all in black, monstrous. It was time to go. Without even asking for the bill, I grabbed Sophie's hand and made a beeline for the door, pushing aside anyone who got in our way. Maybe this guy *is* someone, I probably shouldn't have been so rude. I had no experience of offending large men like this.

We'd driven to the nightclub and there was only one exit from the car park onto the street. The men had seen us go into the car park so went directly to the exit, which was considerably closer than the car. We were trapped and now quite scared. I turned the ignition and could see that this man's bodyguards were standing shoulder to shoulder, blocking the exit. Two options crossed my mind at this point. Get out of the car and try to reason with my long-haired friend and hope that he'll order these people off me. Or pick up some speed in the hope that they'll move. Surely they wouldn't take a car for this guy.

The first option seemed more reasonable but I had no idea who this guy was. Perhaps he was incredibly dangerous and I'd already overstepped the mark, which would mean being beaten badly in a dark car park. Or worse, killed. In either case, were I to get out of the car Sophie would be taken and I couldn't allow that to happen. Second option it was, then.

I put the car into first gear and over-revved the engine as if to warn the gentlemen standing by the exit that I wouldn't be stopping – and floored it. We were reaching the top of second gear by the time we arrived at the gates and the car had picked up some considerable pace. Sophie was screaming with her hands covering her eyes, which I have to say didn't help matters at the time. They weren't moving nor did they look like they were going to move. As we approached this man-mountain I was beginning to question whether or not the car would withstand the accident, but as previously mentioned I had no choice. The men dived out of the way with inches to spare. I felt like I'd just got away with murder, in all senses of the phrase. We raced back to the hotel, relieved everything was over – or so it seemed. As we lay in bed it suddenly dawned on me that I wasn't the hardest person to find on St Barths. If this man was as important as he seemed, I could expect a visit any time in the next few days. Turned out to be sooner than that.

About an hour later I heard loud voices in the corridor about four rooms down from us. There was a lot of banging on doors, people were being woken up, and I was about as frightened as I'd ever been. The knocks got closer and the voices got louder, until they were outside our door. Sophie and I were lying under the bed at this point, almost exactly like a scene from *Taken*. Our hearts were thumping uncontrollably. We ignored the knocking and the shouting – they went away and everything died down.

'Remind me to shave my head in the morning,' I said, before getting into bed.

We couldn't sleep much. The curiosity was overwhelming. Who *was* this guy? The club hadn't closed yet so I called my friend who owned it and asked him.

'Oh what, the big guy with the bodyguards? That's Gaddafi's son.'

A chill ran down my spine.

'What, Gaddafi the terrorist dictator?!'

'Yeah, him. He asked about you actually.'

'And you fucking told him my name?!'

'No, I just told him you owned the Eden Rock. Why, what's the big deal?'

'Why the fuck do you think I ran out of the club without paying, you arsehole! Look, in future if any terrorists ask for my whereabouts don't fucking tell them!'

Excuse the language but in this particular case I thought I'd give you an accurate description of the conversation. As you can imagine, I was pretty het up.

Although I'd been joking with Sophie about shaving my head, having discovered who the man was I decided it was actually quite a good idea, so I did – much to my mum's dismay.

'Oh, your lovely hair,' she mourned. I think she'd prefer to lose the hair than the son.

The disguise was tested several days later when Beyoncé

was singing at Nikki Beach. The Band had mentioned earlier that day that he might be heading over there for a drink in the evening and that I should wander over for one or two. I agreed. On arrival at Nikki Beach, I ordered a drink from the bar and scanned the crowd looking for Dad. I saw him chatting to some guy in the VIP area so made my way over. As I drew nearer I began to notice that the man he was speaking to looked alarmingly like the guy who'd tried to kill me a few nights before. At that point I tried to bolt but it was too late. The Band was waving me over.

'Spen, Spen,' he was shouting.

He doesn't know my name, he doesn't know my name, I thought as I sheepishly made my way over. Prior to shaving my head I had longish hair, easily long enough to put into a ponytail – although I never did. My appearance had altered drastically and I really hoped he wouldn't recognize me. My final hurdle was whether or not Dad had broached the subject of the Eden Rock yet as that may have caused sparks to fly. But The Band never boasted about his achievements and I highly doubted he wanted this man staying there anyway, even with no knowledge of the story.

I shook hands with Gaddafi's son, said hello and goodbye almost instantaneously and borrowed my dad away to the bar. The Band had previously found my head-shaving to be 'a bit of an odd decision' thinking it could be because Brad Pitt had just done the same, but once I offered up my great escape story he found it all the more amusing.

That was the last time he or I ever spoke to Gaddafi's son, may he rest in peace.

CHAPTER 16

When Spenny Met Maxy

At the end of my work experience in St Barths, I spent a short time in Europe snowboarding with some close friends, my last bit of freedom before attempting to tackle a serious job in London. Returning to London felt good. I had enjoyed my time on St Barths but it's a small island and I was beginning to suffer from mild cabin fever. It was the right time to move on and I was looking forward to living in a cosmopolitan city with a host of different people. Despite this, and the fact that London and St Barths are very different places, as soon as the plane touches down in either one, I feel a sense of homecoming.

James kindly invited me to live with him and also asked his City mates to check for openings for trainee traders or suchlike. A job came up at a specialist brokerage firm, where I would assist in selling financial products, mainly CFDs (contracts for difference). Work began almost immediately. I was the only person who was not from Essex apart from the head of the desk, Andrew Turnbull, who was Scottish, and Max Keble-White at the end of the room. Max turned out to be a friend like no other. It took four or five days until we spoke but even before then I knew we'd be close. He controlled his side of the room in an effortless manner and seemed good at everything that he did.

Corporations in the City, as juvenile as it may seem, often have 'initiation' processes for new people much like sports teams and frat houses. In this case, it came in the form of four Big Macs, four large chocolate muffins and four cans of Stella. Henry and Ben – who were also new boys, both from Essex – and I were led into the conference room where we found our food stations. The entire office had put money in a jar, all notes, and had placed bets on who would be able to consume everything in front of them the quickest. The winner was to split the money with everyone who backed them. Because I was posh, very few people backed me, in fact only Max did, which meant that we'd split the winnings fifty/fifty. Being competitive public school boys, we knew we'd won before I even started. Challenges like these have always been a forte of mine and I wasn't about to lose in front of a new crowd. The competition started and I began on one of the burgers in a fairly normal manner. When racing amateurs, you can always be safe in the knowledge that they will eat as quickly and as much as possible straight from the start and inevitably become full, bloated and slow long before the finish. This was a case of the hares versus the tortoise.

One of the beers was used to wash down the burgers, leaving me the muffins and three of the beers. The other boys were ahead but physically strained. They had both decided to tackle the muffins first – a tactical error – so whilst they were battling with their burgers, I rolled my four muffins into four just over bite-sized balls and finished them pretty promptly. I was now easily ahead, and enjoying my beers safe in the knowledge that all I would need to do, should anyone come back into contention, was simply to down the remaining Stella. My brother Mike taught me how to open my gullet at a young age so this was never going to be a problem. I finished the last of the drink, enjoyed a wink from Max and went back to my desk whilst the other two battled it out for second place. Adam Richman would be proud.

Max and I pocketed more than we would have earned that day and then hit the town together. This would be the start of one of the most meaningful relationships of my life. We had a lot in common and formed a brother-like bond almost immediately. After work we'd regularly go out and experience everything the City had to offer. There's this buzz in the City; it's rife with people looking to unwind after what was either a great or an awful day – often it made little difference. Max and I liked being surrounded by these people: men in suits and ties, and women in pencil-skirts and 'secretarial' glasses, hard-working successful people who enjoyed spending. Everyone can get bored of their job, but you can't get bored of that kind of energy. The City will always be this way.

From pub sessions, we'd frequently progress to bars, then clubs, and then afterparties before heading straight back to work. These jaunts were often led by heads or desk managers, or even senior management – seasoned pros who were hard to keep up with, at least for some.

It's very difficult not to like Max. He looks you in the eye and shakes your hand firmly and is the kind of person whose opinion really matters. Everyone needs five minutes with Max. He really pays attention when you speak, never seems sidetracked and always has your best interests at heart. Back then, these attributes were noticed by women all over London. He had a way with words and a level of confidence that proved difficult to compete with at the time. Some men find it easy to charm a girl into bed by making her feel special, but for Max it was almost effortless because he is so genuine. I was never quite sure how he did it but he had a talent for escalating certain situations, like getting girls – even ones who to the untrained eye would appear rather prudish – to undress and kiss each other on the kitchen table, all without seeming to have done anything. He's a lover of women and life, and a great rounded character. Max has an open invitation to anything I do.

I've always admired Max's love of adrenalin and adventure. He is incredibly active and enjoys hurtling through life. You name it, Max has done it. He frequently throws himself off the world's highest gorge jumps, and would revel in any sort of record attempt or challenge. His only real fear would be losing those close to him. He's extremely family orientated, like I am.

Max had once taken some of his friends skydiving in Seville and had passed his accelerated freefall licence while there. Claiming it was a fantastic life experience, he said that we should go together so that I could pass mine. I enjoyed racing fast cars and riding fast bikes but I really wasn't sure about throwing myself out of a plane. Also, tandems are not part of this course, meaning that at no point would I have anyone professional secured to my back doing all the work. Max explained that he'd never done a tandem either and it wasn't a problem. Of course, this made it fine . . .

We arrived in Seville and I began my training on the ground. This was a series of tests regarding safety and the equipment and what to do in case of an emergency, or chute malfunction. We were looking at the kind of malfunctions that happen once in every ten thousand jumps. Or so they say. We also learned how to adapt our position to fall through the air in a safe manner and how to jump out of the plane and become stable quickly. This ground school takes place for a whole day, and then you are briefly tested prior to making your first jump the following day. We sat the written exam at about 4 p.m. on our first afternoon, and due to the fact that all this information was to be quite important, most people did very well and passed the test. As I wasn't particularly looking forward to my first skydiving experience, I had paid particularly close attention and happened to pass the exam with 100 per cent. After all, it was a matter of life or death.

Max had been jumping all day as he progressed to the next stage of his skydiving licence. There were only a few loads left to go up when I wandered over and told Max that I'd passed with flying colours and was looking forward to jumping with him tomorrow.

'Jump with me now!' he said.

I explained that this wasn't within the regulations and as I didn't want any preferential treatment, maybe I should just sleep on all the new information and jump tomorrow. Max looked across the room and in his usual manner called out to the owner of the operation and asked if I could join the next load.

'Yeah, if he's up for it,' the owner said. I wasn't happy with this.

'See, mate, no problem,' Max said cheerfully. The decision had been made for me. I was going up then and there. Prior to this moment, I was the guy on a commercial airliner who, when faced with any sort of turbulence, would grip his seat and grimace. I've never been overly fond of flying so the next twenty minutes were going to be a challenge to say the least.

Before I knew it, we were climbing steeply in a rather small aircraft that seemed to rattle very loudly. I was kitted up with a lot of equipment that was still unfamiliar. We arrived at 15,000 feet and the lights went from red to green as the plane door opened. What seemed to be freezing cold air came gushing into the plane as the reality of the situation became more and more apparent. The people sitting in front of me were gradually moving closer and closer towards the open door.

When you're standing by the door, you only have a few seconds to jump as each person has their own target to hit. And yet, if it's your first time, everything in your body and mind is urging you to remain in the plane. It seems such an unnatural thing to do – to throw yourself out of an aircraft – but at this point everything happens so quickly that it's just too late to stop and argue the point. Almost everybody freezes when it's time to jump, and the staff at these kind of companies are fairly used to this stalling, so they give first-timers a little help – in the form of a rather unsympathetic shove, in my case.

Suddenly I was airborne and approaching terminal velocity. Fortunately first-timers are joined by two professionals who offer up some assistance if required – keeping the client stable or helping them to pull the chute if they are too panicky or stressed to find the toggle. I managed to completely forget all the training I'd had while safely on land. I couldn't remember where anything was or keep my body in the calm state required to fall in a stable manner. The staff later described my first jump as 'wrestling a bull' whilst falling at 125 mph towards the ground.

Surprisingly, one of the scariest moments of the first jump isn't leaving the plane; it's the seconds immediately after pulling your chute when you're completely alone – and in the unlikely event of a malfunction, would be handling it on your own. They say on the ground that once your chute is pulled you should give it a long four seconds before looking up to check that the canopy is properly open. When one is trying not to die, it's often quite difficult to wait for those four seconds. Like so many before me, I looked up too soon and met with what appeared to be a flailing mess above my head. Death suddenly became all the more imminent. If given time, the chute should open properly, which was true for my first jump. A splendid moment indeed. As my adrenalin levels dropped to something approaching normal, I found it was possible to take in the beautiful Spanish scenery.

Skydiving is a wonderful – but terrifying – experience and it's quite rare to look forward to one's second jump. In fact, on landing, most people feel a strange mixture of gratitude – I'm alive! – and anger – I *paid* for this? For some, the first jump is enough, but as the company in question did not offer refunds for the remainder of the course, and given that I'm not one to waste money, Max and I enjoyed some sangria and agreed to return to jump the following day.

Waking up the following morning was harder than I'd anticipated. Despite being told that skydiving becomes easier and more enjoyable once you overcome the fear, I really hadn't had a good experience on my one and only jump so far. Still, I thought it was worth persevering and fortunately there was a different feel as we arrived at the airfield this time; it was less threatening, I suppose because I now knew what was in store, and felt more comfortable tackling it. The opening of the plane door will always be a slightly disheartening moment for me, but the next few jumps were indeed a lot easier. Once you become comfortable in the air, there is no greater feeling than flying. Coming to grips with the way your body can change direction, pivot, flip, even slow down, is fascinating. I imagine it is truly like being a bird.

Max and I were having a great second day, as he'd anticipated, but then on our final jump something went wrong. I was in the same cargo as Max, and had jumped first, meaning that I would be on the ground to watch and welcome the rest of the guys as they came down. Once on the ground you can just about make out canopies opening as people pull their chutes. Max was one of the last to jump, and when he pulled his chute, it soon became apparent that he was spinning in an unusual manner. He was falling fast with his chute open and he appeared to have little to no control. Max was going to have to put into practice those hours of training to save his life. He was going to have to cut away from his primary canopy and deploy his reserve – something none of us on the ground had seen before. The chute pinged off him like a detached sail in the wind as he went back into free fall, only a few thousand feet above the ground. We felt helpless, but I knew Max had it in him. He pulled his emergency reserve cord and fortunately it deployed quickly and perfectly. He was safe.

When Max landed he seemed the most excited he had been all weekend, claiming that he had absolutely loved the experience of overcoming a major malfunction. It certainly didn't put him off skydiving in the future. All in all, it was a great trip. I left with an accelerated free-fall licence and Max had advanced with his. To this day we both love jumping out of planes and flying has become much easier.

Once back in London work at the brokerage firm became monotonous. Many of my friends were out enjoying life a lot of the time and I felt quite young to be submersed in the financial industry. It was nice having what many would call a serious job, but although I wanted to make money and prove myself my heart wasn't yet ready for life behind a desk. Salvation came in the form of Alex Webb.

The first time I laid eyes on Alex, I was quite taken aback. He was standing on a table in Amika nightclub, which was popular at the time, surrounded by gorgeous people. The whole club seemed to revolve around him. Alex defined cool and looked like a character from *Risky Business*. He was pulling off a backwards cap, and dishing out vodka to girls from a jeroboam – a large bottle. These cost an enormous amount of money, but it would later become clear that not only was Alex not paying for anything, but the club was in fact paying *him* to be there. A concept that I had no idea existed.

Alex and I clicked instantly. He found my level of interest in the nightclub industry positive and potentially useful to his company, and asked me to join him. At that time he had fallen out with some of his partners and was looking to rebrand what was then Veneer Parties. Like many club promoters today, it was Veneer's job to ensure that parties were full, had good music and were generally memorable. Alex's parties revolved mainly around his love of house music and they were easily the best nights in London at the time. It wasn't long before Alex and I were the only two people running Veneer – now Veneer London – and we had managed to form links with many great London clubs that are still open at the time of writing.

Within the first few weeks, Alex and I were earning more money a night than I would in a month at the brokerage firm, and so it came to pass that I left the City and became a professional nightclubber, a job which particularly agreed with my nature. Meanwhile, Max moved to work at ICAP, the world's leading interdealer brokerage, and we kept in regular touch.

At one point Veneer was throwing six regular nights a week, giving Alex and me just the one night to enjoy outside of nightclubs which we usually spent . . . in a nightclub. We had officially become vampires and the light of day was rarely witnessed. The constant hedonism was taking its toll on our health, but we were having fun and didn't really care, particularly not while we were doing so well, having been awarded 'Best Promoter' at the London Bar and Club Awards two years running.

Expansion is key to any business and in order for us to expand we needed more manpower. We were a few weeks away from Halloween and wanted to throw our largest party to date. It would fall on a Friday, our favoured Amika night and where all the magic had begun initially. We did, however, have one obstacle to overcome – almost a thorn in our side – and it came in the form of my then nemesis, Harrovian Mr Hugo Taylor.

Hugo was extremely popular in London at that time, as he still is today, and although he swung in similar social circles to Alex and me, for whatever reason we had never seen eye to eye. There was an ego clash to say the least. He was far more outspoken then than he is now. It had occurred to Hugo, as it had to many other intelligent young men and women at the time, that club promoting was a very easy, quick way of making money if you could move a crowd. Hugo could certainly do that, but we were competing to bring in many of the same people, and this was counter-productive for both of us.

Hugo was holding his Halloween party at Boujis and was making quite a lot of noise about it too. Alex and I were of the opinion that having two subpar events running on the same night wouldn't help either company, so through gritted teeth I accepted that we should ask Hugo to work with us. We offered him a trial on Halloween, which was our way of acquiring all of his guests, and to sweeten the deal we offered a higher fee than he would have earned during the night without us, with a view to keeping him on afterwards. Something which, I have to admit, I had no intention of actually doing.

Hugo agreed and the Veneer Halloween party at Amika was of astronomical proportions. We brought over six hundred people through the door and sold every table. There was no specific moment when Hugo and I became as close as we are today, but the turning point was definitely during that night and we've not had any differences to speak of since then. The energy in the room – which we were both responsible for – was just so perfect that we were brought together as if by default. From that night on we were glad to have Hugo working with us and it wasn't long before we were all equal partners in the company. It was a definite case of 'if you can't beat them join them'. Alex, Hugo and I became an unstoppable force in London's clubland.

I enjoyed some of the best nights of my life while running Veneer. Of course, we were all revelling in single life, and many girls came and went, but every so often I'd meet a showstopper who I knew was more meaningful than the rest.

It was during one of these Veneer nights in Whisky Mist that I first met Louise Thompson. Over time, I have discovered that I don't really have a type when it comes to girlfriends but back then she was all I could have dreamed of. She was petite and slender with beautiful big eyes. She seemed innocent yet sexy. I knew then and there that we had to be together. I found her fascinating and we got on famously. We shared a kiss that night and had lunch the following day which turned out to be the first of many. I longed to be with Louise but, given my age and current profession, holding down a serious relationship seemed near impossible. Despite seeing her all the time and caring about her enormously, I just couldn't trust myself. I was in temptation's way on a nightly basis and would hook up with other people, as I'm sure she did too. But although we both pretended to be cool with it – as long as we were honest with one another – this kind of relationship rarely works and someone usually gets hurt. We decided it was best to split up.

In the meantime, Veneer was still running strong. One of Hugo's responsibilities was to source young energetic guys to provide some of our weaker nights with a bit of new flair. This is when I first met Mark Wright, who did a bit of work with our Wednesdays at China White. Mark is a nice, competitive guy and is usually good at whatever the job in hand may require. He later went on to be the lead character in the ITV2 show *The Only Way Is Essex*, shortly before we started filming *Made in Chelsea*. It was amusing to both of us that we were frequently compared in the press as similar characters in different shows. We've never really spoken about the fact that we worked together in the past.

Alex's family has a lovely villa in Portugal where Alex, Hugo and I decided to take a break from 'work'. We were going to play golf, eat healthily, develop nice tans and detox from what was really becoming an all-too-regular party lifestyle. We didn't see a golf course once.

On arrival we enjoyed some of Alex's dad Phil's finest wine by the pool and one thing led to another. Soon we were gallivanting round Lagos (affectionately nicknamed Slagos by some) in search of a good time. We found a lovely little Portuguese restaurant with a terrace overlooking the town. It was quite pretty actually, despite all the rumours I'd heard about the place. Hugo was particularly intent on getting loose, so we did. We then stumbled across Whytes Bar, which had a fairly threatening-looking shots contest. With over a year of Veneer nights under my belt I thought it would only be fair to step up to the mark. The challenge was to drink ten double shots of various alcohols, some of which were mixed together. All of the favourites were included – vodka, tequila, sambuca, rum – with a few oddballs thrown in such as Baileys, Kahlua, etc. The rules were that every drop must be consumed and that there was to be no spillage. I remember looking at the leader board and being somewhat unimpressed with the time of the Samoan in first place – around 16 seconds.

'What's the catch?' I asked the barman.

'You put 100 euros on the bar, and if you lose, you lose your money, and you have to pay for the shots. If you complete the task, you get your money back and the shots for free. And if you break the record we give you 100 euros.'

'No, I mean why did the Samoan guy take sixteen seconds? Isn't that a bit slow?'

He told me to put my money where my mouth was. Which I did.

My alcohol tolerance has always been alarmingly high and no matter how juvenile it may sound, I've always prided myself on being able to consume large amounts quite quickly. The barman rang a bell to get everyone's attention, so all eyes were on me by the time he was ready to start the stopwatch. Suddenly I began to think that this might be a little harder than anticipated. These pre-challenge jitters disappeared as the shots slipped down in just over seven seconds. They were disgusting but I was happy with my performance. The barman handed me my winnings, and the boys and I sat down. I didn't feel too bad at this point, although I was beginning to realize that my victory would be short-lived.

Those who know me well know that one of my pet hates is being told that I can't do something. So when Hugo said that he was impressed with my time and knew I couldn't possibly do it any quicker than that, he got me thinking that I could. It's a trick he often plays on me – and as usual I fell into his irritating trap. The 100 euros went straight back to the barman and the shots were lined up once more.

The second time didn't go so well. I was quicker initially but knocked over the last shot meaning that the time wouldn't count and I'd consumed another nine large shots for no reason. So I was now worse off, as I had to give back the 100 euros and pay for the shots for failing to complete them – and cope with being quite drunk. Alex and Hugo found the whole thing hilarious. The sensible plan would have been to quit while I was ahead – lesson learned.

The next thing I remember is hurtling down the motorway in the back of a car, hoping it was being driven by one of the boys. And then nothing . . . I woke up in my room at the villa the following day with absolutely no recollection of anything in between.

To the best of my knowledge, several years later my record still stands.

Back in London we found that the promoting scene was changing – and our hold on it weakening. Club owners were finding it more economical to pay many different individuals a sum for every person they brought into the club, rather than to pay set fees to companies such as ours. Retainers, such as the ones Veneer were invoicing for on a nightly basis, started to dry up. We understood the club game by this point and thought we could attempt to control external promoters from within the clubs. Thus we decided to move in house at several venues: Alex accepted a job at the Brompton Club, Hugo took a PR job at Bourne Capital and I took a PR and marketing manager job at Movida at the end of 2010. It was there that I met Funda.

CHAPTER 17

St Tropez Summer

The dancers at Movida have always been renowned for their beauty and talent. Around the time I began working there, the dance troupe was run by a company called Beautiful Performers, which was owned by a Miss Funda Onal. As well as organizing the Movida dancers and other events in London and beyond, she also performed and danced herself and, in my opinion, stole the show on a nightly basis.

It was immediate infatuation. Funda was one of the most beautiful women I'd ever seen, older than me and seemingly unobtainable. Unlike the other girls I'd felt this way about, Funda knew exactly what she was doing, and I was in her control from the very first time we met. Occasionally she would enjoy herself, in a friendly way, by playing on her position of power. Everything I thought I knew about women had become irrelevant. Even my bosses Marc Merran and Eamonn Mulholland were telling me to dream on and not to bother – which, of course, made it more worthwhile.

As I knew we would be seeing each other most nights, I thought it best not to rush into anything or to risk making work awkward. So I purposefully paid Funda very little attention to begin with, in the knowledge that I was willing to go the distance.

This plan backfired quite dramatically on one of my first nights working at Movida, when I thought I'd test the water by kissing a fairly promiscuous-looking club girl within eyeshot of Funda while she was dancing. It was no secret to those working in Movida that I had a bordering-on-weird obsession with Funda, so they thought it was a fairly odd move on my part. I just wanted to see if she cared. And much to my delight – and ultimate disappointment – she did. Realizing that I may have a chance, it didn't take me long to ask her out. But at this point she was convinced I was a womanizer and kept bringing up the meaningless kiss. I tried to explain that in a strange way I'd done it for us, but she wasn't having any of that. I'd taken a few steps back and for the following weeks was on my best behaviour. It became something of a joke but deep down she must have known that I'd just made a stupid mistake to get her attention.

A few weeks later, I'd had several particularly strong nights out in a row and had absolutely nothing left in the tank. I'd been drinking just to get myself through work and was spent. I couldn't wait for the club to empty out so that I could go home and sleep. That's when Funda came up to me and asked if I wanted to have a drink with her. Funda never drank at work, not even at the end of the night, so obviously it was significant and I accepted. She then went on to say that she and the girls were heading out to Jet Black, an after-hours club, and I should join them. Of all the nights she could have asked, she chose this one, probably having noticed that I was completely wounded. I think she wanted to test whether I thought she was worth it, and of course she was, so I went.

This was the first time that we had socialized outside of work. I didn't care that it was in Jet Black. We were spend ing time together in a normal social situation which was a step in the right direction. A few weeks prior to this outing Hugo had nipped in to see me for a drink or two in Movida and I'd made him aware of my interest. He approved. I texted Hugo saying that I was heading out to Jet Black with Funda to which he simply replied, 'Just do your thing, man.' He's always had a very simple yet effective manner when it comes to advice.

I managed to find form on arrival at this second club and things quickly started to fall into place. Asking myself why Funda had invited me, I could only assume she felt some sort of interest. This opportunity could not be missed. We were sharing a table upstairs with the rest of the dancers and some other friends when the urge to kiss her got the better of me. I was aware that she was either having complications with a boyfriend or that she was recently single, neither of which I particularly cared about at that moment. As I leaned in with my eyes shut, I was met with two fingers on my lips. I opened my eyes to her smiling as she whispered, 'Not here, it's too public.'

I immediately experienced a sense of victory and knew I couldn't wait much longer. Having envisioned this moment for weeks, it now seemed to be right here. There were large black curtains behind and surrounding the table, and noticing that no one was really paying us much attention, I swiftly engulfed the two of us within the swathes of cloth. People clearly knew what was going on but at least we were no longer in public. My heart had been in this for a while and I wanted to make a grand gesture so Funda would realize how much she meant to me. It was the perfect romantic moment and certainly the best night I've ever spent in Jet Black. I texted Hugo on the way home and he was delighted for me.

Work became more enjoyable, although we kept things between us relatively quiet at first. Of course, some people knew but the majority didn't. We still hadn't spent a whole evening together but if it meant having her in the long run I was happy to take things slowly. We'd share moments at work and briefly kiss in back rooms, but we both had jobs to do and finding any quality time together was difficult.

Funda had slight reservations about making our relationship – or whatever it was – public as she had only recently split from her ex-boyfriend, who also worked in the club sector, and was conscious of his feelings. After all, she does have a heart of gold. It took a while for her to go on an actual one-on-one date with me. I think she was wary of entering another relationship and was therefore keen to keep things between us fun and casual. Although one night she did agree to allow me to cook for her.

I'd had lots of experience working in restaurants and tried to come up with something tasty and impressive. I had a word with her best friend at the time and fellow performer Emma who informed me that any attempt to impress her with over-the-top culinary techniques would not work. Like The Band, Funda is from Sheffield and being a good Yorkshire lass the easiest way to her heart would be through the old favourites. So Emms and I agreed on steak and mash and banoffee pie for dessert. However, even after taking the complexity out of the menu, it still needed to be perfect. So I called in the best chef that I know to do pretty much all the work before Funda's arrival – my mother. I laid the table and Mum did everything else bar cooking the steaks which I thought I'd just about be able to manage myself. The hostess, a device used to keep food warm without drying it out, was full of delicious home-made food by the time Funda arrived. Obviously I'd put the dirty apron on and Mum had vacated the premises.

I was living with James at the time, who happened to be out that evening so we were on our own. The house was a beautiful, mainly underground open-plan modern building. It was truly the perfect setting. We cracked open a bottle of red and our first date went really well. She was particularly impressed with my cooking and to this day doesn't know that I had very little to do with it.

Although we had to go to work after dinner, it was after

this night that we began spending real time together. As far as I was concerned, she was my girlfriend from then on and I wanted to take our relationship seriously. It wasn't long after we'd established ourselves as an actual couple that I received an amazing job offer – running Papagayo nightclub in St Tropez for the summer. It was well paid and obviously the idea of being in St Tropez was very appealing. Funda was very career-orientated and agreed that it was an opportunity not to be missed, especially at my age. After some consideration I decided to take the job and told Funda that I would fly her out to stay with me whenever possible.

It didn't take long to fall in love with Funda whilst I was away from her in St Tropez. Despite being with close friends, Megan and Richie Williams, who spent much of the summer there, I had completely lost my usual urge to approach women when out. In fact, the only thing I could think about was Funda. No matter who I met or how many drinks I'd had it was simply impossible to get her out of my mind. No sooner had I been there for a week than I called her, confessed my love and offered to fly her out for a few days.

We spent some quality time together in St Tropez, and it felt so right that I was having trouble imagining the summer without her. One evening, while I was dealing with an issue in the VIP room of Papagayo, I noticed the dancers on the podiums behind the DJ booth. It suddenly struck me that they weren't much better than the beautiful performers in Movida. In fact, I wasn't sure they were better at all. What could be so wrong with them that we would need replacement dancers? My devious mind got to work . . . but I found nothing. Instead I just went straight through the front door. I met with the owner the following day.

'The dancers are subpar,' I said.

'What do you mean?' he said. 'They're great.'

'No, they're not,' I replied. 'I thought you hired me for my opinion on details such as these. Trust me on this one, they are subpar and I can have a suitable team out here to replace them almost immediately for the same money.'

He took my advice and allowed me to make the arrangements. I hadn't spoken to Funda at this point about whether or not she even wanted to take the job, but I was young and in love and all I cared about was getting her to St Tropez. Fortunately, she seemed keen on the idea and, after some negotiations with the club, she and her troupe were on their way out. I now had the dream girl and the dream job for the summer and was in my element. The only thing I hadn't told Funda yet was that we'd be living together. I wanted to assume she'd just take that for granted. I only discovered recently, years later, that she found that to be a particularly bold call of mine.

I was sharing a house with the four dancers: Funda and I were in one bedroom, and the three other girls were in the other. Needless to say I'd kept the shabby housing arrangements to myself in the knowledge that once they arrived it would be too late to go home. It took the girls several days to warm to me again. I pleaded ignorance, obviously.

It was arranged that Funda and I would have the same evenings off and we'd spend this time dining out at some of St Tropez's most beautiful locations. Chez Christina was a particular favourite of ours and it was there that she first told me she loved me back. Despite all the complications with the living arrangements, it really was a summer that I'll never forget.

Since we were working at night, we had time during the day to enjoy ourselves. Club Cinquante-Cinq for lunch was another favourite, arguably the most famous beach club in St Tropez, with tables booked up months in advance, and people arriving by boat as well as land to eat there. It serves the most exceptional steak tartare – if I had to eat just one dish for the rest of my life, their steak tartare with chips, a green salad and vinaigrette would be a strong contender. When we were lucky, we sometimes spent afternoons with my sister Nina and her brilliant children Lily, Rosa, Jasmina and my partner in crime, the great Tristan, either on their boat or around the harbour-side townhouse that Nina and Adam had bought bang on pitch overlooking the artists busy painting the beautiful view. Funda is still a popular topic of conversation amongst the kids.

By the end of the French interlude, Funda and I had gone from strength to strength and as soon as we were back in London, we moved in together.

I was over the club game at this point, and the idea of

spending every evening in a nightclub while living with Funda was not what I wanted. She was focusing more on her modelling career and far less on her dancing, so in an ideal world we would have liked to spend our evenings together. Funda and I were both of the opinion that going back into finance would be a good call for me at this stage in my life – and of course my friend Max was at ICAP. It is incredibly difficult to get a job at ICAP and you can't just walk in so I looked at another company also owned by Michael Spencer, City Index. The premises were just across the road from ICAP and I thought a job there would be the ideal opportunity to get a foot through the door of his empire. I was interviewed by some top class guys and fortunately they offered me a position. The work was similar to that of the brokerage firm and I was directly across the street from Max.

It was only a matter of months before a position became available within ICAP, and with a lot of help from Max I was put in the running to compete for the job. Weeks later and almost out of nowhere I was sitting next to Max on ICAP's US Dollar/Swiss Franc desk headed up by Adam Nelson and Michael Schmid, two very different yet equally colourful characters. This job involved exciting trading every day and a whole spectrum of finance that I was eager to learn about. It was riveting and I enjoyed every moment of it. I had landed the perfect job in the City, working with my best mate.

*

I'd been working at ICAP for nearly a year when I got the call from Hugo, who said that a production company wanted to discuss the possibility of us appearing in a TV show. Given the economic climate at the time, I have to say I wasn't particularly interested in becoming the laughing stock of Great Britain but figured we might as well go to a meeting.

For the most part I thought this meeting would lead to disappointment or time-wasting, but I knew I'd feel foolish if the programme were to fly and I hadn't at least entertained the idea of getting involved. Hugo and I tried to play it cool and act as though we weren't particularly interested, but gradually as the meeting went on and it became increasingly clear that this show was going to be made, we struggled to contain our enthusiasm.

Work at ICAP carried on as usual and I was careful not to mention the show to anyone other than Max. He was sceptical and thought that abandoning a job at ICAP to appear on a television show that might flop after a few episodes wasn't prudent, particularly not when we'd put so much effort into securing my job in the first place. I'd watched other reality shows and had always found them uninteresting and bland.

Any filming I did would have to be okay with ICAP as I didn't want to risk losing my job in the City. That meant I was faced with the rather difficult task of broaching the subject of appearing on television with ICAP. I reassured them that filming was a hobby, rather like fishing or painting, and that the show would probably amount to nothing and certainly wouldn't affect my work. They consented.

We started filming the first series of *Made in Chelsea* in February 2011 and I have to say Hugo and I were excited, mainly due to the opportunities that this could present in the future. Neither of us were shy characters and we believed that we could make a great show. *TOWIE* had taken the nation by storm and we thought that eventually we could do the same.

In the first scene we filmed together we were driving in my beloved black Land Rover, en route to a party at Raffles – of course. At this point we didn't know how the show would turn out. It's difficult to speak your mind when you know you're going to be judged, in addition to which we had no idea how we were going to come across. If you re-watch the first few episodes of season one, there are a lot of awkward silences and many people being extremely careful about what's said. For example, I knew that every single thing I said to Caggie would eventually be seen by Funda, and vice versa. Hugo would ask questions about Caggie, for example, and I felt I couldn't be completely open because I wasn't just speaking to Hugo, I was speaking to everyone who was watching. This caution didn't last long.

When we shot our first group scenes together at Raffles, I wasn't quite sure what to make of everyone. On first meeting Mark Francis, I thought he seemed a little insensitive towards anyone who wasn't wearing Gucci and didn't drive a Bentley, and I had doubts as to whether or not the show was for me. When he declared, 'Chelsea girls don't eat,' all I could picture was being a laughing stock amongst the British public. Mark is like Marmite: you either find him hilarious or simply don't understand him. He is a complete one-off eccentric and has become one of my favourite people on the show. Two things I respect about him are that he always speaks his mind and he dresses exceptionally well.

I hadn't seen Caggie for a while as I'd been with Funda for over a year, and was very happy in my relationship. But for reasons unknown, whenever I've spent any time with Caggie all the feelings that I developed at a young age are impossible to block out. Even then I realized I was likely to be at the centre of a lot of drama in the show.

CHAPTER 18

In the Beginning

I never thought it was possible to be in love with two women at once – or to end up losing both of them.

Until the start of *Made in Chelsea,* I was in a good place with Funda. I really thought we were in it for the long haul. But when Caggie reappeared everything changed. I kept bumping into her, this stunning girl who for some reason has always had a hold over me. Almost immediately I was in a real predicament. I had everything I wanted and more but for some reason I just couldn't ignore the love that was denied to me as a schoolboy.

Looking back, I can see how it must have seemed as if I was treating Funda badly, but everything was quite confusing at the time. When at home with Funda I would occasionally think about Caggie – I couldn't help it. I never meant to hurt Funda, but every time I met up with Caggie and filmed with her I just seemed to fall in love with her all over again, and I began to think I wanted to be with her. Of course I also wanted to be with Funda . . .

Filming the entire first series of *Made in Chelsea* whilst still working for ICAP was particularly challenging for me. I would get up at 4.45 a.m. every morning for work and then have to spend most week nights filming until late as well as all weekend. This made it very difficult to have any time for anything else and it began to be a strain on my relationship with Funda. We started to argue over the pettiest of things – I suspect due to a lack of sleep – but it made the prospect of being with Caggie all the more attractive.

I never spoke to Funda about my feelings for Caggie because I didn't know whether they would break us up, or whether they just weren't important in the long run. For all I knew, Caggie could leave my life as easily as she had reappeared.

One of the most commonly asked questions regarding the show is 'Is it real?' and the answer is yes. The content of the scenes and the friendships and relationships are entirely genuine. The stories you see played out on TV are organic and show what is going on in our real lives.

Maybe this is why the whole Caggie thing became so central to the first series. I would wear my heart on my sleeve and tell Hugo about my infatuation. I became used to the cameras so quickly that I neglected to hold things back. I was even filmed telling Caggie that I was confused about our relationship, and that I had strong feelings for her, fully aware that when the show hit the air in a few weeks the nation, including Funda, would be watching. Perhaps the truth doesn't always come out immediately but it needs to in the end. Being on a reality show, it's only fair to be real. If you make mistakes or have genuine feelings for people, you should speak about them, giving everything you can to the show. This certainly doesn't make you popular in many cases but it is worth watching.

Finally, the first episode aired on 9 May 2011 on E4. All of us involved in the filming gathered together to watch it. Seeing ourselves on TV was quite foreign. Why none of my friends had given me a heads-up about my appalling hairstyle will always be a mystery. Fortunately, starting with slicked-back City hair meant that I was only ever going to look better. It took a short trip to see the fifth love of my life, Jennifer Manzi, at the Daniel Galvin Junior Salon in Belgravia, to sort it out just in time for series two. I was really happy with Jen's work; in fact, once you've had long hair and you go short you always ask yourself what you were thinking before. I know this is certainly true of Ollie Locke. One young lad, George Penny, was such a fan of my transformation that he regularly drives all the way from Cardiff to see Jenny for a similar cut to mine.

Obviously watching yourself on the show can be quite awkward, especially when the gloves have come off or bitter truths have been spoken and the person who has uttered them is sitting behind you. During that first series, the tougher moments for me were when my feelings for Caggie began to air whilst I was still with Funda. But Funda, being as beautiful and confident as she is, didn't feel threatened at the time and didn't make a big deal of it.

I have always been proud of what we create and was delighted when we began to realize that *Made in Chelsea* was becoming a success. Its viewing figures were growing – and continue to grow. And it now shows in many different countries, including the USA.

I've always found it funny the way programmes such as ours can influence a slightly younger demographic when it comes to strange ways of talking. In fact, just as *TOWIE* introduced words like 'well jel' and 'reem' into the nation's vocabulary, *Made in Chelsea* has a few of its own. I was enjoying a day at Wimbledon recently, despite the fact that Roger Federer got knocked out by someone who has since been forgotten, when I heard from the other side of the court a voice yelling, 'Yeah, boi!' – a saying that Jamie claims is his, although he knows it's definitely mine. The next step is stealing 'old sport' off DiCaprio's Gatsby for series six.

The drama I was experiencing with Caggie was putting a strain on my relationship with Funda whose patience was being severely tested. We were falling further and further apart. ICAP and filming was becoming a lot to juggle and I was tired, run down and not feeling like myself. We got to that horrible place in a relationship where we would almost prefer not to be around one another, but when you live together in a one-bedroom flat in Putney there are only so many places to escape to. The general consensus from friends, particularly Hugo, was that the relationship had run its course and that I should spend some time being single and try to enjoy myself a bit.

Funda and I broke up not long afterwards. Fortunately James had plenty of room at his, so I was able to move out quickly and effortlessly. The following few weeks were sad times for me but in retrospect it was undoubtedly the right thing to do.

After our break-up we didn't talk for about eighteen months. That is a rare thing for me as I've always been good friends with my exes. I've never seen a reason to dislike any of them; if we wanted to be close in the first place then there was something special between us – and that doesn't just disappear following a split. Staying friends seems to be the natural thing. After time, and once everything had blown over, Funda and I were able to become close again. If she ever needs anything, she knows she can always call me.

After Funda and I split, I let Caggie know that I was still interested. By this I mean I took her to the South of France with our best friends and led her to a nice little spot with a beautiful view and told her that I'd loved her for the past six years. Hugely unsubtle, far too full-on, bordering on desperate. Needless to say this didn't work. Caggie has always been a bit deeper than what can only be described as my enormously uncool and over-the-top gestures. It helps to be actually going out with someone before going all in.

CHAPTER 19

A Real Life Gatsby

Being in the public eye unfortunately makes you a bit more attractive to the opposite sex, as many of us in *MiC* soon learned. With the success of the show, we became minor celebrities and our lives changed. Some handled it well, some not so well. We were invited to all manner of showbiz events and film premieres. We were popping up everywhere. These parties, despite all being a bit similar and repetitive, can be fun. There are usually unlimited free drinks, good food and the occasional goody bag. Being newly single, it was fun not to have to worry too much about the girls who were not backwards in coming forwards.

The reaction towards me from the public was pretty favourable at the time, which is always pleasing. 'Spaggie' was widely spoken about in the press and the will they/ won't they storyline began to dominate the first series.

But having overcooked it again, this wasn't going to be my time either. Instead, I enjoyed a new friendship with the beautiful, funny and smart Chloe Green, daughter of Sir Philip Green, CEO of Arcadia Group, which includes Topshop, BHS and Dorothy Perkins. I met Chloe out and about and thought she was the most lovely girl. She told me she'd seen some of the show and regularly pulled my leg about it. We hung out, having a laugh together, had dinner in nice restaurants and just enjoyed life in general.

My favourite place to eat in London is Japanese restaurant Zuma, a place Jamie and I frequent far too often. One of my favourite spots in the world, however, would have to be Michelangelo's in Antibes, called Mamo's by many. Mamo's is in a converted stone-walled wine cellar and although it is quite expensive it isn't pretentious in the slightest. The Italian food is splendid, the atmosphere is great, and best of all it's a family-run restaurant. Mamo heads up the kitchen whilst his son controls the floor. It's particularly hard to get a table around Cannes Film Festival time as word of this restaurant has spread over the years. One of my more memorable moments at Mamo's was in fact with Hugo, Caggie and Millie. Caggie still raves about it – the restaurant, that is.

But back to Chloe . . . She very kindly invited Hugo, myself and a few of our friends to Monaco to join her family on their yacht *Lionheart* for the Monaco Grand Prix weekend. I've been fortunate to fly on private jets a few times but I have to say that Sir Philip's is especially beautiful. When the plane door opens and the stairs leading onto this wonderful aircraft unfold, I always make a note to self to work harder.

Two particular moments from that weekend come to mind . . .

The first was a lunch that Sir Philip had arranged on the yacht. I was sitting across from him. My godfather Alex Lees-Buckley, who had brokered the deal for Sir Philip to buy the *Lionheart*, was also there that day. I wasn't sure Sir Philip had warmed to me as he didn't seem to care too much about what I was saying. He did, however, turn his attention to me, albeit for a moment, to ask what I thought of a certain football club, the name of which escapes me. I'm more of a rugby fan myself but was vaguely aware that the team in question definitely wasn't a front-runner. I replied that I knew nothing about them, and they were probably shit – I thought that was what he wanted to hear. He then went on to tell me that the gentleman sitting to my left, who was also part of the conversation, owned the team and that I should talk to him about it, before wandering off. Fortunately, the football chairman turned out to be charming and rather humorous himself.

The second memorable thing took place on Race Day in Monaco. Sir Philip and Lady Tina had invited lots of people onto the boat. Hugo and I made an effort to look as good as we could on little sleep. For Hugo this involved pulling out one of his more expensive items, a new cream knitted cardigan by Ralph Lauren. The garment would crop up in conversation far too regularly, as Hugo was extremely proud of it.

'Maaate, how high end is this Ralph cardy?' was dropped several times throughout the day.

'Fine.' Short one word answers did the job to keep him at bay.

Drinks flowed and everyone was having a great time relaxing and chatting in the sun. It wasn't long before some very familiar faces were gracing the boards of the deck – designers, actors, models and other interesting, colourful people. Perhaps the most celebrated guest was Mr Leonardo DiCaprio. At the time he was with Blake Lively and they both seemed like lovely people.

A little later, as the heat was coming off the track, a few people were playing backgammon at the front of the boat, by the pool. Leo was on one of the boards, and appeared to play quite well. Glass in hand, I waited for an opening and it wasn't long before I was sitting opposite the Great Gatsby himself, enjoying one of my preferred board games. We played a few games and were of a pretty similar standard. Leo had a very nice way about him. I honestly can't remember who won or lost. For the sake of the story we'll give the victory to him – however unlikely that may seem.

More time passed and more fun was enjoyed. Chloe suggested a change of location and a small group of us got ready to leave. However, Hugo's cardy was missing and this meant that Hugo was going nowhere. He searched the boat high and low, before getting a team of people to help him. Chloe's remarks that it would be kept safe once found were falling on deaf ears. Eventually he spotted it . . . The reason nobody was able to find Hugo's cardy was because Leo had found it and was using it as a cushion. I was surprised by Hugo's hawk-like vision as Leo was in fact sitting on most of it, leaving only a minute patch of cream to be noticed.

Hugo approached Leo. 'Do you mind? You're sitting on my cream cardy.'

Leo turned and looked at him with this air of puzzlement and as he moved to free it said to Hugo in an American drawl, 'Who the hell calls it a cream cardy anyway?'

'An Englishman,' said Hugo, clutching his newly creased cardigan protectively.

I had another opportunity to visit Monaco shortly after this trip when, in June 2011, I accepted an invitation to drive in the Dodgeball Supercar Rally. This is a five-day drive across Europe with stop-offs and entertainment in various cities. That year we were to head for Zurich via Venice, Monaco and St Tropez and I couldn't wait.

I was driving with my mate Manny, a City trader who has now become a regular client at Eden Rock. All of the drivers involved met in London the night before we were due to depart and this turned into quite a big party for some. So much so that when Manny pulled up the following morning to start the journey I was really wishing that I'd had some sleep. The car was beautiful, a new and stunning matt grey Lamborghini Diablo costing around £220,000. No sooner had I familiarized myself with the car's interior than I dropped off. Not very good company, I know, but I needed a quick rest, even if it was only for an hour or so.

We'd barely made it out of London when it began to

rain. I was waking up and nodding off again fairly regularly down the motorway. On one awakening it felt like we were doing a casual 150 mph. The road was beginning to get quite wet now. The next awakening wasn't quite as gentle. Manny had lost control of the car due to the sheer power of the beast and the wet surface of the road. Suddenly we were aquaplaning down the motorway, spinning full rotations, bouncing off the barriers, taking out two cars in the process before coming to a halt.

We were very lucky that there were no large trucks or vans nearby; the motorway wasn't that busy thankfully. The car was completely totalled but Manny and I were both unscathed. One of the other drivers got a bit of a nasty knock but nothing serious. That was it – Manny and I shook hands, I got a taxi home and our supercar rally ended right there and then by the side of the M20, only thirty miles from London.

Meanwhile, the relationship with Chloe had also ended, but with significantly less drama. We remain friends and we all enjoyed having her on the show in *MiC*'s second season.

Before the end of the first run, and despite not being a hit with everyone, the show's popularity was unquestionable. Twitter in particular had some fairly impressive figures. When we are on air, the show receives anything up to 250,000 tweets an hour – outdoing popular shows such as the *X Factor* and *Britain's Got Talent*.

I was particularly looking forward to the upcoming

second season because two of my best mates, Jamie Laing – who I'd become close to by this point – and Oliver Proudlock, had both agreed to do the show. They both asked if I thought it would be a good idea for them.

'Should I do it?' Jamie asked on a night out.

'Definitely! Of course you should. It will be great for your profile, amongst other things,' I told him.

'So, will I get laid?' Jamie wanted to know.

'Yes, even you.'

'Done, I'm in!'

That was an easy one. Proudlock was slightly more hesitant. He has always been careful about the decisions that he makes in life. His primary concern was that he would be perceived as a reality TV personality and that it would affect his up and coming, and now very successful, clothing range Serge DeNimes. It has always been important to Proudlock to be taken seriously. After endless discussions he began to see that publicity and a higher profile couldn't possibly do his brand any harm. He would have to mess up in a pretty major way to do that, which isn't really in his nature – he's too clever.

Also joining us was The Porg (person of restricted growth), my ex, Louise Thompson. I can assure all of you that this is an affectionate name which she loves and in no way has this ever been bullying. Her brother and close friends also call her Porg or Porgie.

As soon as I started spending time with her, I realized the attraction was still there. At this point, I'd given up on Caggie because after telling her that I loved her, she'd told me yet again that she didn't want a relationship with me. This had become all too familiar, and it was around this time that I began to let go of those dreams of Caggie and I being together for life. Funda once said to me that if Caggie wanted to be with me, then we'd be together – and she was right. Louise and I didn't want a full-blown relationship at the time but we were both still attracted to each other and enjoyed one another's company so decided to be friends with benefits. It seemed to be working out well for us, until Christmas.

A bunch of us went to Finland and everyone seemed to be getting along fine. But then Caggie turned up to surprise us all – and sure enough, everything changed. It was great to see her. She was the only thing missing at the start of that trip.

On her arrival, I offered to show her where she was staying and carried her bag. The setting was beautiful, the snow was thick and white and the air crisp and clean. Once we'd dropped the bag we walked back towards the lodge. Caggie has always had an ability to sense when part of me has moved on from her. I don't think I'll ever be able to fully move on, which is worrying unless I marry her, but there was something about our interaction which was different this time. I wasn't as keen and transparent. We were walking shoulder to shoulder when she slipped on some ice and grabbed my arm. We both went down quite hard although she managed to use me to break her fall, how I'm not quite sure, but it worked out fine. We were lying in the snow together, laughing. It had been such a lovely evening that we stayed outside for twenty minutes or so and shared the most meaningful kiss we've ever had.

Was this the night I was going to make love to the woman of my dreams? The night all my dreams were going to come true? In part, yes. It's no secret that many of us are not averse to a drink and when on holiday in Finland, drinking is something of the norm. Jamie, Caggie and I were particularly poorly behaved having drank the hotel's entire vodka cellar. We've all been drunk many times but this was something completely different. The vodka was so freezing that it slipped down seamlessly. We must have had a couple of bottles each. Drinking games, forfeits in the freezing cold, it was savage.

When Caggie and I eventually made our excuses, probably in sign language by now, and left we just about made it back to the cabin. Had I known that the seven years of waiting was going to come to an end then and there I would have prepared better. Perhaps drunk rather less . . . It was like a bad comedy in some ways, but nonetheless it was an important milestone in my life. The following night was exactly the same. And then it was time to go back to London.

Caggie and I didn't need to speak about our relationship on our very special trip to Finland; we both knew the score. It was a holiday fling and the end of a chapter. Things felt different in a good way, almost like a weight had been lifted from my shoulders. It was as if there was no more pressure on me – she was free.

CHAPTER 20

Sketching

After so much emotion with girls I decided it was time to concentrate on mates. I have always had a few more male friends than female ones. My boys are really important to me, and I had neglected them of late. Just before we began filming for series three, I had a chance to show one of them exactly how important he was.

Max called while I was in the middle of a photo shoot for the new series and said, 'I'm off to New York for a few days to see my buddy Jack Houston. Why don't you come? He's a cool guy and it'll be a good laugh, and it means I'll actually get to see you for a bit before you disappear off to film or whatever.'

Max knew I would have loved to have gone but unfortunately I just didn't have the time.

After hanging up, I couldn't stop thinking about how good this trip would be. As it happened, and by pure coincidence, I had my passport in my back pocket. I checked flights out of curiosity and there was one that didn't cost too much that was leaving in three hours. Decision made.

My flight was set to leave an hour after Max's, so I'd be following him over the Atlantic, stalking him without his knowledge. I called his sister to find out where Max was staying and she was very helpful. On arrival at the hotel, I swiftly found out which room he was in just before being informed that he'd nipped out for half an hour or so. This couldn't have been more perfect. I asked for a key to the room, which of course they didn't give me but I did have the room number. So instead I waited outside the room until a maid came by and said that I'd been locked out and needed to get back in. She obliged. I was in. Now all I had to hope was that Max didn't suddenly have a change of heart and stay out.

Max scares easily. I'd turned out all the lights and positioned a chair in the centre of the room facing the door. I then proceeded to call Max, seemingly from the UK, to apologize for not being able to travel and to make plans for when he got home.

'What are you doing right now?' I asked.

'Nearly back at the hotel. I'm going to freshen up and head out.'

Excellent, I thought. I was trying to work out what to say or do once he opened the door to make this experience as horrific as possible, and settled on just saying nothing. It would be darker, more sinister and disturbing in the long run. I heard the key go into the card reader. I was excited. It was on.

Max came into the room alone and flicked the lights on. And strangely enough didn't see me immediately. It took him a few seconds to look around the room but when he saw me, he saw me. The noise he made was alarming. I'm not sure if you're familiar with the term 'sketching' but Max sketched in a pretty major way. I don't think he spoke for the next twenty minutes. Too much for the mind to handle, I take it.

He got over it eventually and we were happy to see each other. The trip to New York was indeed excellent.

Once home in Chelsea, girls were back on the agenda. But the course of true love never did run smooth and I realized that my feelings for Louise had changed yet again. With Caggie now on the other side of the world – she had gone to Australia to work on her music – I had no distractions, and started to think about Louise in a romantic way again. The only problem was that by the time I had come round to this way of thinking, Louise was being pursued by Jamie. This was a bit frustrating. Seeing her with someone else made me re-evaluate things, as it tends to – when your best friend goes for your ex, you can't help but wonder what you're missing and I guess you become a bit competitive too.

What was worse, Louise was responding to Jamie's advances. She seemed to enjoy his attention and looked like she would be keen to at least give him a shot. It was torture seeing this because I had persuaded myself that Louise should now be with me again. And I believed that deep down she would rather be with me than with Jamie . . .

Hugo, Millie and I went to Dubai to celebrate Louise's birthday. Jamie stayed in London as he was busy with work and was a bit short of cash at the time. I think they were going to figure out whether or not they wanted to be a couple once she got back from Dubai. I still believe Jamie wasn't losing any sleep over it. While we were there, I made my feelings very clear to Louise. I wanted her to be my girlfriend. As I had hoped, she felt the same way and we began what was to become one of the hardest relationships of my life.

Jamie didn't take this well, but in my opinion he was milking a sympathy vote. If Jamie had given me genuine reason to believe that he wanted to commit to Louise and be her boyfriend, I would never have done what I did in Dubai. Ninety-nine per cent of the show's fans took his side and Louise and I became public enemy number one. The fans' reaction was understandable. Jamie is much loved and he deserves to be. He's such an honest and open enthusiast, a top man and a top mate. Fans had invested their time in our love triangle. But the online comments that came piling in were vile. Some were urging Louise to kill herself for stamping on Jamie's heart, while other tweets were beyond crude. I've never minded reading negative press about myself, I've often found it quite amusing, but some of these comments, particularly to Louise, were quite unnerving.

What got me through were some wise words from a

senior executive at NBC Universal. He told me that in shows like *Made in Chelsea*, it's more important to be memorable than to be liked.

Once Porgie and I finally got together properly, life was grand and I was loyal to her. I enjoyed being with Louise and we really got on famously and for a good while.

It's a relief when filming for a series finishes, as it usually becomes pretty intense towards the climax. The end of this one was a little different because it would be Hugo's last series. He was always the person who supported me and made me feel better about stuff and I knew I would miss him.

I still see lots of Hugo and his girlfriend, little Miss Natalie Joel, who I know to be the love of his life. We call her The Good Bengal because she's usually well behaved and she looks like a pretty little Bengal cat, as does her twin sister Karin who I may or may not have dated.

One of my good friends Tom Montgomery-Swan – great name, I know – races powerboats professionally and was a founder of Vector Offshore Racing. One weekend, the owner of a team a few categories below what Tom's used to asked a favour – would he step in to cover for a driver who had unfortunately broken his arm a few days prior to a race? As this would effectively be the equivalent of go-karting for Tom, he thought it was a great opportunity for me to experience my first powerboat race. This isn't to say the boats were slow. In many ways this kind of racing is more dangerous than the top level as the safety equipment is less advanced.

When we arrived at the boatyard, I spent a while eyeing up all the boats we'd be racing against. Some seemed sophisticated, some less so. Ours fell into the low-end category. In order to co-pilot for Tom it was necessary to sit a health and safety exam demonstrating that I was familiar with the equipment and was comfortable with power-boating in general, which of course I was not. Tom practically sat my test for me and before I knew it we were in helmets, neck braces and life jackets and set to hit the Thames.

As soon as the race started, it was clear that Tom was easily the best driver there. Despite our boat having worse lines and being less powerful than those of our competitors, we were right up there at the front. One would assume that racing a boat is fairly straightforward, but the amount of physical effort required to hold a straight course was impressive. The weather conditions were not bad but the water was certainly not flat which boded well for Tom. Typically the more experienced, courageous drivers prevail in conditions like this.

My job was to keep an eye on surrounding boats and inform Tom whether or not it was safe to hold his racing line – a collision could be fatal, these boats were going over 100 mph.

The race had been going for around an hour and we were approaching our final lap, fighting for the lead, when we came into some unexpected cross waves in a bend at high speed. The boat rocked in a dramatic fashion and despite Tom's best efforts to counter the effect of the imbalance we barrel-rolled at top speed. On impact, the seats were torn from the boat while we were still in them, and we were pushed deep under the water. In the moment that the boat flipped, I believed that was the end. I won't say that my life flashed before me but there was a definite point when death seemed imminent. We had been told prior to the race that if these boats flip at high speed there is limited chance of survival and now we were living it.

The impact itself didn't seem painful at the time. The pain came later. The whole thing happened so quickly, I didn't quite lose consciousness but it took several seconds to understand that I was still alive. The shock and near-freezing temperature of the water were all in all quite confusing. I could barely see through the visor of my helmet. There was no light to speak of. When the turbulence of the impact calmed, I went to swim for the surface and that's when I discovered I could only move my legs. This made swimming to the surface quite difficult. I could only kick and was wearing heavy boots. I was also winded, and as I was fighting for breath, there seemed to be a good chance that I was going to drown.

It turns out you can always hold your breath for longer than you think, if necessary, and eventually the buoyancy of my life jacket brought me to the surface. All that I wanted was to take my helmet off but given that I couldn't move my arms I was going to have to wait helplessly. At the time I thought that both my arms were broken and the pain was immense.

I was in complete shock but suddenly it occurred to me that I wasn't the only person in this crash. Tom was nowhere to be seen. I thrashed around to try and find him and saw him about ten metres away face down in the water, motionless. Getting to him would be a problem but, like so many well-organized races these days, the safety boat was on point within a matter of seconds. Tom's unconscious body was hoisted safely out of the water and he was strapped to a stretcher and secured. Tom was dealt with first as I was quite clearly conscious and therefore less of a priority. In fact, given that I was being fairly vocal it was clear that the impact hadn't finished me off so they spent about ten minutes tending to Tom whilst they let my pain well and truly sink in.

The thought of having two broken arms didn't bode well and I was still fighting to use them. In doing so, and with the help of water resistance, out of nowhere my left arm snapped back into place and felt normal almost immediately. The pain was still excruciating but at least I could use my arm. I began thinking that perhaps my right arm wasn't broken either and tried frantically with the use of my left hand to pull and push it to see if it too could find its socket. It took longer than the left one but eventually I managed to relocate the right one too and I was able, albeit carefully, to remove my helmet which at this point was making me extremely claustrophobic.

When the paramedics eventually turned their attention

to me one of them seemed to have misheard the information about my shoulders and went about dragging me onto the boat by my arms. As anyone who has dislocated their shoulders will know, the muscles surrounding your sockets are loose for a little while afterwards and your arms can slip in and out fairly easily. Being tugged doesn't help matters and my right arm was pulled out again. I was already in so much pain that I barely noticed, but it still didn't make me particularly happy.

Once in the boat all eyes were on Tom, a trend which continued for hours after the crash. When we arrived back on the bank, I was sat in the back of one of the spectators' cars and given a small towel and a whisky; Tom, now conscious, was being tended to by fifteen to twenty people within full view of the crowd. If I didn't know any better I'd say he was enjoying it. Meanwhile both my arms were falling out whilst I was trying to dry my hair with the tea towel, unattended. Once the shock had passed and I'd managed to warm up I got out of the car and went to join the many people looking after Tom. It was as if I wasn't in the same boat, literally. I asked Tom if he was all right.

'Fine,' he said blankly, as he was being lifted into an ambulance.

I almost had to ask if I could go too. Tom got the bed, I got the seat that your mother would sit in, and we were off to the hospital. I was still in extreme pain, but Tom seemed quite content. On arrival at the hospital, Tom was carted immediately to the emergency room, while I was asked to take a seat by the Coke machine. I was genuinely under the impression that the entire world had gone mad, or that I was just having a bad dream.

'I was in the same fucking boat!' I protested to the medical staff. 'I can barely feel my upper body.'

This was news to the hospital attendant, and I was eventually given a bed next to Tom. Tom realized he was receiving preferential treatment, but found it quite funny and so allowed it to continue. We got scanned: he was unscathed, I was 'informed' that my upper body was in trauma – a fact that I was fully aware of. We were given tuna sandwiches and told we could go home after a doctor offered to strap both my arms up, an offer that I declined given that I thought it might impede me being able to do anything. I accepted one sling so that I could swap it depending on which arm felt better at the time.

When we were discharged from hospital we nipped back over to the boatyard briefly for a quick drink with the rest of the guys from the race and were told that the commentator, over the loudspeaker, had informed parents with small children that they should perhaps lead them away from the stands as this kind of crash could often be devastating and to expect the worst.

Sleeping was hard for a while, as my arms came in and out as they pleased. Tom has since asked if I'd like to go boating with him in a more leisurely manner, but so far the idea has not appealed.

CHAPTER 21

The Bachelor

Things were going well with Louise but, as always seems to happen, I began to feel restless. Louise is a stunning, intelligent girl but greatly dislikes being alone. She needs someone to be by her side constantly which can get a bit claustrophobic. Any arguments usually stemmed from issues of minor importance, which was also irritating. She agreed, albeit reluctantly, that we needed some time away from one another.

Channel 5 was casting for a second series of *The Bachelor*, the British version of a smash hit US TV format which had previously starred rugby ace and ex of Charlotte Church, Gavin Henson. I'd never watched *The Bachelor* but from what I could see Gavin seemed a genuine guy and took the show seriously and people saw a different side to him.

When I heard I was being considered, I was surprised, as I wasn't as high profile as Gavin, but I was quite excited too and thought that meeting a nice girl who I may not otherwise encounter in my day-to-day life might be exactly what I needed.

I knew it would be unfair to keep Louise in the dark about a job offer of this nature so I spoke to her about it. She was of the opinion that it would be good for my career and a great opportunity for people to see a different side to me. So we agreed that, however unlikely, if I got the job, I'd accept it. After some back and forth with Ricochet production company and having tried to ignore rumours of my competition, they made me an offer and after some negotiation I was to be Channel 5's next Bachelor.

I don't know whether Louise expected that I wouldn't get the job but she certainly didn't take it as well as she thought she would.

Before signing I did raise the point that the chances of me finding the love of my life on a reality television show in which girls compete for the attention of a man that they've never met were pretty slim, but I'd try my best to be charming and gentlemanly and hope that they'd made some interesting choices.

What I was looking for on *The Bachelor* was a girl with a sense of humour who I could have a laugh with but who was also honest, modest and patient and would take easily to my pace of life. Of course, a girl being good-looking always helps too and no one can deny that's where the initial attraction develops, but for any chance of a proper relationship, those other character traits are crucial to me. What I wasn't so keen on were girls who overdid it with the make-up and hair extensions. I'm more of a natural beauty person and don't fall for women with fake tan and too much make-up.

Before starting on the show, people thought I'd have a problem if some of the girls were from different backgrounds to the girls on *Made in Chelsea*. But that was not so and never has been with me. People are people wherever they come from. Not only that but let's not forget that The Band came from Yorkshire and I'm proud of the fact that he has worked hard to give his family a great life. I've dated a wide variety of girls from all different walks of life and I certainly don't care about their background or how much they have in the bank. It's the character that counts.

Filming began in the South of France, in a lovely big seafront villa. On the first evening I had to stand at the top of a red-carpeted staircase, candlelit by the pool. I knew what to expect on some level as I had just watched Gavin's first episode. I was far less nervous before doing so. What was nerve-racking wasn't meeting the girls, it was living up to their high expectations. Presumably if you've been chosen to do this show you should be the perfect bachelor and I've never once considered myself that. These girls were probably expecting someone credible at least. Every time I'd been in love I knew it was going to be a special relationship from the first moment I'd met the girl. There has always been a very distinct spark and although the spark is in many ways superficial as you don't know the person, it still helps to have it. I was hoping for that spark with one of the twenty-four girls who were about to get out of their limos. There's no question that many of the girls were attractive but I didn't have that sense of love at first sight with any of them. This was certainly going to be a very interesting process. Over the next ten weeks, we would have to speak in depth about our feelings and by the end of the show one of these girls would be my girlfriend. Daunting stuff.

While I enjoyed observing behind the scenes on *The Bachelor*, I was out of tune with most of the girls. There were a couple, like Khloe, for example, who I looked forward to seeing on-set, but the majority just weren't my type. I missed Louise while I was away. It's true what they say – absence really does make the heart grow fonder. But romance aside, I did have some good times with the new production team and many of the girls were a lot of fun.

As time went on, I began to really like two of the girls, Tabby and the eventual winner Khloe. I have often kicked myself thinking that I should have chosen Tabby, but at the time picking Khloe seemed like the right thing to do. She was fun, energetic and had a really great natural way about her. Speaking to the two girls individually at the final rose ceremony in the Bahamas was an experience that I wouldn't wish on anyone. Effectively, I'd been dating both these girls for ten weeks and now I had to break up with one of them. But I liked both of them. I'm bad at breaking up with people, that's why I rarely do it. By now you'd think that I would have learned my lesson and digested the fact that straight talking is the best way forward but it's never that easy. I remember my conversation with Tabby on that final filming day quite vividly. Breaking up with someone when they've done absolutely nothing wrong feels awkward. The only thing that feels more awkward is breaking up with someone because you fancy the girl she's been living with for the last ten weeks.

By the end of filming, I was pretty dated-out. Unless you were offering me a dried fruit from the Middle East, I didn't want to hear the word 'date' for a while afterwards.

After the last show, Khloe and I were contractually obliged not to be seen out together for eight weeks until the final episode had aired on TV. When I returned home, Louise and I met socially with friends as I kept an eye on the rules of the show; I was looking forward to being able to spend a bit more time with Khloe as of course all of our meetings and dates up until that point had been on camera. It would be good to get to know the real Khloe away from the competitive atmosphere that had developed during our time on the show together. It seems, however, that these feelings weren't reciprocated as one night young Khloe had a few drinks too many and slightly overstepped the mark with Tom Pearce, one of the guys from *TOWIE*. It wasn't a very big deal and it's something that I could have probably overlooked but to do it publicly like that just sent the wrong message and I wasn't of the opinion that she deserved a second chance. Tom and Khloe went on to date for a while and in many ways they are definitely better suited.

*

As soon as I was contractually clear, one of the first things Louise and I did was meet up in St Tropez. I'm a big fan of spontaneous, short holidays. It is not always cheap, but then I have never been one for hoarding my money. I want to gain pleasure from it with a girlfriend and friends. If I have saved £2,000 to last a month and I go into a club and end up spending £1,000 and then have to live leanly for the rest of the month, it doesn't worry me so long as that night was great and felt worth it to all of us. I'll happily pay for friends to go out to somewhere expensive for dinner and drinks, particularly if they don't feel they can afford it at the time. Oddly enough, the real value of these moments often comes back to you, with other people being generous in return, offering you a special 'in' somewhere good, for example. But not always – and I admit to having gone over the top a time or two when the testosterone has kicked in too heavily!

One evening in St Tropez, Louise and I had a table in a club called VIP Room with five other friends, and I had ordered a bottle of vodka for us to share. On the next table was a guy called Alexis Stellakis, a friend of Jamie Laing's. While we get on now, Alexis and I have had our differences and we brushed each other up the wrong way that night.

I saw him look over at our vodka and pointedly order the same, but in magnum size. So I ordered two magnums, then he got another. It was a ridiculous 'lad-off'. And so I decided to end it by going straight to the ultimate choice on the menu – a methuselah of champagne, which of course is a single bottle that holds six litres, the equivalent of eight bottles. It was Moët and cost £3,000 and was so heavy that when it arrived it slipped out of my hand and sprayed Louise. It was ridiculously showy of me, everyone was looking, and there was no way we were going to drink it all, but I still felt like I had won. Until the sober morning after when I had to call the bank and reason with them! The only way I was able to console myself was in remembering that it had been Moët – to put it in perspective, had the bar sent something like Dom Pérignon, the bill would have been more like £20,000 and that would have been me done for, good and proper.

CHAPTER 22

The Slap

Following *The Bachelor*, I was more than pleased to be back in London and with a new series of *Made in Chelsea* to film. The show was doing better than ever. The third series had reached over a million viewers so the show was really beginning to make its mark, just as its predecessor *TOWIE* was on the wane.

Andy Jordan also joined the new series and much to my annoyance was running around after Louise. We developed a natural rivalry quite early on and, of course, when it came to Louise, I had to step in and make my feelings clear. He became a thorn in my side and his persistence was never short of baffling. In retrospect, I don't blame him as persistence is a particular trait of mine as well.

I began to focus attention on ways to use the doors that *MiC* had opened in a business sense. My outlook on business is innately optimistic and I have always assumed I'm going to make millions even though I've rarely thought about how to achieve this in the long term. Some of my plans have been less achievable than others. In the last couple of years, Dad and James have tried to explain the importance of having a plan as well as a vision, and I have made an effort to understand the nature of business and develop more entrepreneurial nous. I value the opinions of my father and brother above all others when it comes to money management. They set a good example for me – one that I do always intend to follow. It is in the Matthews' nature to work hard and remain active in order to succeed. Despite having run a couple of marathons and the occasional bit of gyming, my natural appetite for nightlife has often meant that I'm not quite firing on all cylinders when it comes to being as productive as possible – something that I'll no doubt grow out of at some point. My parents provided good schools and homes, but brought us up in the knowledge that they weren't going to leave us trust funds or vast inheritances. The Band is of the opinion that such promises can often spoil a child and diminish their natural desire to succeed by themselves, making them lazy and out of touch with reality. The Matthews kids have always understood that we are on our own when it comes to financing our lifestyles, something which I have found less than ideal at times!

One semi-lucrative opportunity to arise from *MiC* is that of the PA (personal appearance). PA evenings often entail going to a nightclub, university or bar, and chatting with people and having pictures taken. The pay is okay and they are usually quite fun. It's also a great way to interact with viewers directly and to gauge the popularity of the show, which can be difficult to judge through viewing figures as they can vary from episode to episode. The best bit about PAs is that you get to travel and see parts of the UK, or indeed the world, that you hadn't seen before. Proudlock and I recently returned from a tour of Australia consisting of appearances in Sydney, Melbourne and Adelaïde, all of which were memorable. This is where 'the MP' was formed. Hopefully by the time you read this, you'll understand the reference.

On these PAs certain people behave in certain ways. Many do their time and leave, but others enjoy what the night has to offer and ensure that everyone who wants a picture taken gets one. The *Made in Chelsea* boys lean towards the latter. We're all so thankful for the opportunities that the show has created for us that we're happy to spend as much time with fans as we can. Jamie and I particularly enjoy doing PAs as a double act, having always bounced off each other quite naturally. One memorable evening involved some pretty serious crowd-surfing in Belfast – a feeling we'll never forget. We felt like rock stars, if only for a moment.

In the meantime, series four was wrapping up and we were filming the final episode on a boat on the Thames. In the past, and to this day, when I've tripped up or made a mistake, no matter how big or small, I've usually told someone, often Max or Jamie. Max is a fairly safe bet. Jamie FM is not. On that particular occasion my mistake was that I had been unfaithful to Louise. Unbeknown to me, across the room the news had reached Francis Boulle who had in turn taken Millie and Rosie Fortescue to one side and told them what he had heard. At this time Francis and I were not close and I suppose his loyalties lay with Louise so he did what he thought was right. I don't blame him, although it would have been nice if he'd come to me. Having said that, it would have been nicer had I not made the mistake in the first place.

I was in the middle of inviting Louise to St Barths to join me for Christmas and New Year when Millie strode up to me and started on about what she had just heard. 'I think you owe Louise the truth,' she declared. When cameras are rolling in a room full of people and you're put on the spot like that it's often difficult to deal with the situation at hand. I wanted to try and spare Louise the humiliation of going through this on national television. I was the one in the wrong and felt awful that she had to suffer. But my taking the defensive seemed to enrage Millie further. I should have expected it, really, but for whatever reason my guard was completely down as Millie delivered the infamous slap – messing up my hair and sobering me up in the process. It was a good hit; no one can take that from her.

On the night I was unfaithful, I was out with Jamie and Proudlock at Morton's following yet another row with Louise. She had gone elsewhere with her girlfriends. Prior to this night I'd been on a health kick and hadn't drunk in several weeks. I'm in no way looking to make excuses here, just stating the facts. It takes a lot for me to get into such a state that I don't feel in control but on that evening the amount of gin consumed was enough to do so. The boys and I bumped into an old flame of mine, a girl I used to see regularly when single in London and New York. It was good to see her and nice to have a conversation with a girl who wasn't having a go at me. One thing led to another and we eventually went home together, albeit in separate cabs. I do feel guilt in situations like these and apologize to anyone that has been appalled or hurt by my behaviour in the past. I am a young man looking to enjoy life and it is never my intention to hurt anyone.

After the incident on the boat, Louise and I went home to talk. Although I did regret hurting her, especially so publicly, in a way I was glad she had found out as there was now nothing else to hide.

Nevertheless, after sleeping on it, we discussed taking a break so we could both get our heads straight. We needed to work out why I had cheated because, as I said before, I don't cheat in a relationship when I am happy, so I took the fact that I had as a sign.

After a couple of days on my own, I asked Louise to join me in St Barths over the New Year, and after three weeks together in the sunshine it became clear to me that we had both now changed quite a bit. She'd become a different girl. She is lovely – and in lots of ways she was still the same girl I fell for – but by this point the trust had well and truly been broken. I can't blame her for this but unfortunately a relationship can't exist without trust. She had become a little needy, wanting to know everything and always finding some small detail to worry about. It was as if she enjoyed living in a constant state of slight crisis. Whereas I find drama exhausting, she seemed to thrive on it. In my heart, I knew it was time for us to break up, but I still cared for her and we'd become reliant on each other's company, and so, as the New Year began, it seemed easier to let things drift on. It became clear, though, that we had tried to mend the relationship one too many times.

I should have been honest with Louise and confessed that I'd fallen out of love with her and just wanted us to be friends. Instead, we were falling apart. One night, I found myself having an afterparty with Sam Thompson and Stevie Johnson at Louise's whilst she was in Edinburgh. I drifted into that now all too familiar headspace and was unfaithful to her for what would be the final time. The location didn't even cross my mind, although in retrospect the fact that it was in her room was hugely insensitive and wrong.

I finally got the courage to break up with Louise in early 2013, which was hard but we knew it was the right thing for both of us. When she started seeing Andy and I was single again, I felt happy, the happiest I had been in a long time. Having tried and failed several times over the years to give a real relationship a crack, Louise and I have come to the conclusion that we work better as friends. We will always have something special and remain close. I adore her family, especially her brother, Sam, who is one of my dearest friends and always will be. He is regularly referred to as my younger brother.

CHAPTER 23

And the Award Goes To . . .

When I first met Lucy Watson, I thought she was a good-looking girl but we didn't see eye-to-eye. She seemed opinionated, but the more time I spent with her the more I liked her. Lucy is actually very sweet underneath her cold exterior. She has quite a high protective wall that has been scaled by few. I was in a good place as a single guy when we struck up what I called a 'casual relationship'. As it turns out, girls, especially Lucy, don't take well to having the time they've invested in being with you referred to as 'casual'. It became apparent quite early on in this 'casual relationship' that I would need to commit on a higher level if I wanted to spend any time at all with Miss Watson. We agreed to put the whole thing on ice and I proceeded with single life. But of course during filming I would see her, sometimes with other men. I didn't much like this. It took walking in on Lucy's date with Alex Mytton to kick me into gear.

I had flown to Barcelona to take some time to just chill.

The break-up with Louise was particularly toxic and I couldn't help but feel that the situation with Lucy had come at a bad time. I called Jamie and asked him to get a cool group together and to join me for some fun in the sun. By this point I was fairly adamant that Lucy should come but Jamie told me that she and Alex seemed to have something good going on. I had heard from a friend of hers that she did have feelings for me so I had Jamie invite them both.

When we all met up in Barcelona, it was clear from the start that there was still something between us. We had a conversation about our future and decided to become a couple. Although Alex took the whole thing really well and completely understood, very few people invested in the relationship. The consensus was that I was on the rebound following the break-up with Louise, which may or may not have initially been the case, but more importantly, that I needed time to be single – a fact which later turned out to be blindingly obvious. Jamie was particularly vehement about this doomed relationship. He knows me better than most, and I wish I'd listened to him when he said that he thought it was far too soon to get into another relationship, and that I was in no way ready to be faithful to anyone. Jamie's advice on such matters is usually pretty good – although this isn't to say he is always right.

Lucy and I did not even properly date before becoming a couple. Our relationship seemed to be moving at an alarming pace – something I found quite daunting at the time. I was very much in single life mode and kept having to remind myself that I had a girlfriend, which I often wasn't able to do. Although Lucy was nothing short of the perfect girlfriend, I just couldn't get myself in the head-space of being in another relationship.

In May 2013, in preparation for our appearance at the BAFTAs for which *Made in Chelsea* had been nominated, Jamie said, 'Let's go and buy new bow ties for the night.'

Selfridges it was, and as we were browsing the higher end brands for bow ties, a midnight-blue Christian Dior dinner suit caught my eye. I'm not particularly in to fashion, as I'm sure you will have seen, but this suit really was beautiful.

'Do you want to try it on?' asked the shop assistant.

'How much is it, please?' I said.

'It is £3,750.'

'No thanks.'

'The colour is unique to this store. They only made seven. Eddie Redmayne just bought one,' he said persuasively.

Damn. I love Eddie Redmayne, I thought to myself before politely declining and continuing on our quest for the perfect bow tie. Jamie and I bought matching velvet bow ties from Yves St Laurent, one of his favourite designer labels – his red, mine blue. But the only thing playing in my mind was the suit. Jamie told me that I might as well try it on as it may look better on the peg or it may not fit properly. The BAFTAs were the following day so there'd be no time for alterations. I agreed to try the suit on, which turned out to be a serious mistake. It fitted perfectly and I was even more fond of it than I had been before, but I just couldn't justify spending that much on a suit. I began to think that were we actually to win a BAFTA it would be a shame not to look the part. I was really doing my utmost to persuade myself that this suit was a necessity. I thought that a phone call to my mother might be the correct play. I don't often ask my family for anything. We're not big on Christmas and birthday presents etc., but mine was just round the corner . . . My mum is just the most wonderful woman and will always be proud of whatever it is that I choose to do and in her eyes being nominated for a BAFTA was worthy of an early birthday present. And so I had my perfect outfit. I couldn't wait for the awards.

The whole night at the BAFTAs just fell into place. It was the first public outing 'on the red carpet' with Lucy as my girlfriend and she looked breathtaking.

Holly Willoughby was presenting the award in our category, and as I'm a big fan of hers, it felt like a good omen. But when the nominees were read out, my confidence started to waver as I considered the strength of one or two of the competition. I doubted for the first time that we would win. I looked up at the stage and the screen and felt removed from it, as though watching from home. The idea that we might be up on that stage in a moment as winners seemed too much to ask. When Holly announced: '*Made in Chelsea*!' up we went and it was a great moment for the whole team.

GQ magazine later voted me one of the top ten best-dressed men on the BAFTA red carpet – making that suit money well spent.

Looking back it is clear that I was not ready for a relationship. I did feel like I loved Lucy, but everything moved far too quickly. She had a set of keys on the third day of our relationship, and from the moment we started going out we were inseparable. Lucy is far more sensible than I am and she never put a foot wrong. In many ways she was ideal but she lacked something, a certain electricity that I find attractive in people. I felt our relationship was somewhat restrictive; it was almost like settling down.

It wasn't long before we said we loved each other, and although I meant every word at the time, I now realize that my heart wasn't completely in it. Most of me wanted to be with Lucy but part of me wanted to be single. Everyone thought I would cheat – and they were right. Unfortunately I just wasn't able to shake the desire to be free, and despite my strong feelings for Lucy, I behaved as if I was a single man.

I felt guilty and wanted to tell Lucy about it. I even had a conversation with Hugo in which we discussed how I should own up to her, but in this instance I thought it would be best to brush the whole thing under the carpet and try to make it work. I believe that people can change but they really need to want to. With social media being so rife nowadays it took little to no time at all for my behaviour to make its way onto Lucy's iPhone screen. She confronted me and I eventually told her everything. I've always respected Lucy's fiery nature and strong woman image. I believe she was disappointed above all because she believed that we would be together for a long time. But she had previously made it clear to me that she was a one strike and you're out kind of girl and I'd had my strike. The break-up was far more difficult for me than I had anticipated. In the past, when I'd made mistakes I'd always been able to claw my way back if necessary, but with Lucy this was not an option. We kept loosely in touch, which was hard given that we both still had serious feelings for one another. But there was just no going back on this one.

Shortly after the break up came Australia, and although Proudlock and I had an incredible time I would often think about Lucy and whether it would be worth even considering trying to get back with her. I felt like a real idiot this time. It took losing her for me to realize how great a girl she was – but unfortunately this relationship is tarnished for life.

I have spent a lot of time thinking about my behaviour and why I tend to end up cheating on those I love. It's strange because, that aside, I believe I treat my girlfriends well. I am genuine and sweet, and always make the effort to check that they are happy and feel looked after. I am not being deluded about this – most of them would tell you that themselves, including Lucy, who once said, 'If you were able to not cheat, you would be the perfect boyfriend. It's a shame.'

I am not making more excuses, but part of it might stem

from insecurity. I have several weak spots; for instance, I have been told I bear a resemblance to David Brent, which can be unnerving . . . Apparently I also look like a pug, although I don't mind that too much, as I like them. In fact, my nickname for many years now has been 'Pug', which I enjoy. Then there is my weight. Ever since I was young my weight has fluctuated and I do put on pounds more easily than I would like. I always live life to extremes, and when I am in party boy mode, drinking and eating to excess, it can creep on quite quickly. I always wait until I'm officially certified fat before taking action. I'll sign up to marathons to give myself an incentive to run or disappear off to a bootcamp somewhere. I've had particularly good results at No1 Bootcamp both in Ibiza and in Norfolk. I've also had great results at W10 Performance in London's Ladbroke Grove.

I'm not such a huge fan of myself – and maybe because of this I sometimes try to prove to my subconscious that I *am* attractive by chasing after girls when I shouldn't.

One day I like to think I will outgrow this juvenile streak that lies deep within me and be faithful to the right person. But at the same time, I'll try not to regret my behaviour too much as I don't see myself settling down or marrying until my mid-thirties. People often ask why I don't just stay single – which I should definitely do – but the truth is that even though so many of my relationships have ended with someone getting hurt, I enjoy the companionship.

*

By summer 2013 I was in a caring yet lighthearted relationship with Stephanie Pratt, sister of my transatlantic twin Spencer Pratt. Stephanie unfortunately lives in Los Angeles, and as neither of us would be able to manage a long-distance relationship, our romance did have something of an inbuilt time limit. But at the time we felt we understood each other.

I was having a drink with Spencer in the UK when he asked me to look after Stephanie on an upcoming visit to London. I was keen to help out but part of me wondered if he hated her, setting her up with me – a brother's worst nightmare.

'You want me to "look after" your sister?' I said, to be sure I'd heard correctly.

'No, I want you to show her round and introduce her to some nice people.'

'Okay,' I said.

Stephanie is a very attractive woman so I knew this was going to be a pleasure and not a chore.

I arranged to meet her for the first time at the Formula One Grand Prix Ball, organized by my good mate Johnny Dodge (who also owns the Dodgeball Rally that Manny and I crashed the Lambo in). From the minute we met there was an instant chemistry. Stephanie is a fun-loving and beautiful girl, and we were close from the off. Having both experienced reality shows (she was on *The Hills* alongside her brother), we understood one another and could talk about absolutely anything, including which other people we fancied. It didn't take long for us to become involved romantically. Stephanie and I both share the same laid-back attitude to relationships.

We didn't need to label ourselves as anything, we were just very happy in each other's company and in no hurry to part. It was an absolute pleasure to be around her and she was widely loved by both family and friends. Then I made a fatal mistake. I didn't want Stephanie to incur the huge costs of living out of hotels in London, so I invited her to move in with me.

Of course, as soon as she'd got her large collection of luggage through the front door she wanted to change me. I was a victim of new girlfriend syndrome. On the pretext of needing some hangers for herself, she proceeded to rifle through the Spencer Matthews Autumn/Winter 2013 collection, discarding any outfit she deemed unsuitable.

'Who do you think you are, Michael Jackson?' she asked, as she held up a leather jacket that, yes I admit, might have had a few sparkly bits on. 'So shocking, honey,' she concluded pityingly.

Originally I was only expecting her to stay a few weeks and as that stretched to about four months of living together, I started to feel claustrophobic. It didn't help that Steph really missed LA, and was finding it hard to adapt to moving in my tight circle of friends, given that they had no shared experiences or associations. We were both suffering cabin fever and the relationship started to fail. We decided to split up, and on the day Steph was going back to LA, Lucy and Louise decided to tell her that I'd been seeing other girls. I realize now that I should have made a clean break before Steph went back to LA, but I felt it was unnecessary to hurt her feelings as we both were well aware that she was going back to America soon and at that point the relationship was going to fizzle out anyway. In my mind the relationship was already over, but Steph was understandably angry and hurt when she found out from Lucy and Louise at their little restaurant rendezvous. As a result we didn't have a very fond farewell and she went back to LA, but she's such a warm, caring and classy girl that I sincerely hope we can stay friends.

With hindsight we moved much too fast from dating to living together and next time I'm going to take things slowly.

Meanwhile, Caggie moved back to the UK in May, and we are still good mates. We occasionally meet for dinner and chat quite frequently. Every time I see her I have an amazing time. There will always be something there.

Made in Chelsea is a great show to be on and it seems to be going from strength to strength. It's hard to believe how far we have come since that first nervy conversation between Hugo and myself at the beginning of series one.

I love being able to film with my friends and the opportunities that have come from being on a successful TV show have been amazing. I've recently set up my own company called Pug Industries, which sells T-shirts, caps and, of course, hoodies. If this takes off, I'll be looking to expand. There are still so many things I'd like to do in the future. I hope to pursue a career in acting one day.

And as for what comes next, there's the new series of *Made in Chelsea* to look forward to and it's brimming with drama so far . . .

Acknowledgements

There are several key people I need to thank for their help in putting together this book:

To my family, thank you for having been there for me over the years. Thanks especially to Mum and Dad for helping me to pull together my memories.

To Pan Macmillan, particularly Ingrid Connell, thank you for offering me the chance to put my life story on paper in the first place. Thanks to Emma Donnan for her help.

To my agent Sean O'Brien, thank you for your guidance and ideas along the way.

Thanks to all the team behind *Made in Chelsea* for the opportunity to be part of the show.

Lastly, but most importantly, to all the fans of the show, thank you for watching and buying my book. I hope you have enjoyed it!

Acknowledgements

Picture Acknowledgements

All photographs are from the author's private collection, apart from:

Page

7 Susannah © Alain Photo

9 Eden Rock – St Barths © Pierre Carreau Ashton © Jesse Grant / WireImage for Think PR / Getty Images

10 The Matthews family © Jean-Philippe Piter

12 Spencer with Funda © Pacific Coast News
Spencer with Louise © Neil Mockford / Film-Magic
Spencer with Millie and Caggie © Pacific Coast News

13 Spencer with Jamie © Retna / Photoshot
Spencer with Chloe © WENN
Spencer with Khloe © WENN

14 Spencer with Lucy © Tim P. Whitby / Stringer / Getty Images

15 BAFTA photo © PA Images
Spencer with Stephanie © Daniel Deme / WENN.com

16 Spencer © Ruth Rose